Overthinking and Anxiety

How to Eliminate Anxiety, Create Productive Habits, Thinking & Meditation, Eliminate Negative Thoughts and Develop a Winning Mentality

Thomas Johnson

Introduction

Congratulations on purchasing this book, and thank you for doing so. This book will help you in understanding the potential threat of overthinking and the ways to avoid falling into its vicious trap.

Thinking is such a powerful process. It has helped us evolve into such efficient and powerful beings. It is due to the power of thinking that we are ruling this world despite being physically weak and inferior to several other races that have existed for much longer than our race. However, like any other powerful process, when it gets out of control, it can be devastating.

It is no wonder that in this age of comforts, we all are suffering our minds to a great extent. We have little control over the things that the mind thinks about. It can easily drag us to negative thoughts and overpower us.

Most people feel helpless in front of their overthinking minds, and this is a reason more than 40 million adults in the US are suffering from anxiety disorders. The count of the victims of other mental disorders in which overthinking and the resulting stress has a definitive role to play is even scarier.

An even bigger problem than this number is the percentage of people who treat overthinking as a problem and seek help. A mere 36.9% of the people suffering from serious mental disorders ever seek medical help. Most people suffering from overthinking don't even consider it a real problem at all.

People believe that it is the job of the mind to think, and if their mind is thinking a bit more, than it is overactive. People don't realize that if more than the required amount of sugar in the blood can be a problem. If more than the required amount of pressure in the blood can be a problem, then why thinking more than the required amount is normal.

This book will help you in understanding all these questions in detail and explain the problem of overthinking in detail.

In this book, I have tried to explain the concept and the causes of overthinking in as simple terms as possible. The root causes of overthinking are not complex, they can be addressed easily, but if you allow the brain to carry on the habit of overthinking for long, recovering can be difficult, tiresome, and strenuous.

This book will prove to be helpful to everyone. Either you have been facing the problem of overthinking for long or feel that you have started falling in the trap of the mind recently. You will get simple, easy, and actionable solutions for the problems you are facing in your mind.

Many people make the mistake of rubbishing or discarding the problem of overthinking as inconsequential. Nowadays, even medical science has proven that the simple-looking process of overthinking can not only lead to mental and emotional issues, but it can also cause neurological disorders. It is a problem that not only affects the functioning of the mind but also affects the smooth running of the body.

This book will provide simple and actionable ways to bring changes in the way you think. It will help you in understanding the ways to modify your thought process and get out of the trap of overthinking.

It will also provide you the techniques to break the deadlock caused by overthinking. It will give you ways to come out of the habit of inactivity and indecision.

This book will introduce you to the effective practice of meditation and the ways in which meditation can help you in breaking the habit of overthinking.

This book will not only provide the basics of meditation but will also give you an in-depth understanding of the practice for countering the overthinking problem.

It will also give you pro-tips to beat the negative thought processes in the mind and gain a winning mentality.

This book is a sincere attempt to help you in overcoming the issue of overthinking and find peace, joy, and success in life.

I hope that you will be able to get the full advantage of this book.

There are plenty of books on this subject on the market, thanks again for choosing this one! Every effort was made to ensure it is full of as much useful information as possible; please enjoy it!

Chapter 1: What is Overthinking

An overthinker is a simple person with a complex mind

Overthinking is the helpless state in which you are unable to stop your mind from thinking about a thing you don't want to think about.

Confused?...

Let us begin with a small but interesting story...

Once upon a time in the far east, a person proud of his mental prowess went to a very famous monk to get the knowledge of mystical powers. He took the recommendation letter from the king so that the monk doesn't engage in dilly-dallying. He wanted the powers quickly.

When the request was made to the monk, he didn't have many options. Acting against the recommendation of the king could prove to be fatal.

But, the monk had his reservations too. Back then, it was a tradition to impart the knowledge only to the deserving. Every teacher had a great responsibility to find the deserving candidate, and then only he could pass on that knowledge. Many powerful teachings are believed to have passed into oblivion because the teachers didn't find the deserving students.

Here was a student who wanted fast delivery of the teachings without having to pass the test of time and merit.

The monk thought for a while and then agreed to impart the knowledge.

He gave that person 3 simple mantras to chant:

BuddhamSaranamGachhami

DhammamSaranamGachhami

SanghamSaranamGachhami

However, there were 3 Very Important Conditions to be followed:

1. That person had to stand in chest-deep water early in the morning to chant these mantras.
2. He had to chant these mantras 7 times
3. He must not think about Monkeys while chanting these mantras

That person felt he was on the seventh cloud. He couldn't believe it would be so easy to get mystical powers.

The monk again reminded him that he must not think about monkeys, or else the mantras wouldn't work. That person assured that there was no reason for him to think about the monkeys.

But, somehow, his thoughts were now getting diverted towards monkeys. The harder he tried to brush these thoughts, the more aggressively they attacked. He couldn't sleep for the whole night thinking about those damn monkeys.

The next morning when he went into the water, more than the mantras, he was thinking about the monkeys, knowing fully well that he doesn't have to think about them. He came out of the water without getting any success.

Soon the thought of those monkeys took over every aspect of his thought process. He simply couldn't shake them off.

He saw those monkeys in everything around him. All his thoughts were simply about the monkeys.

He went running to the monk and pleaded to do anything to get those monkeys off his mind.

He didn't want anything else in this world. He was on the verge of losing all that he had earned to date due to those monkeys that didn't even exist.

This is the kind of effect overthinking can have on a person.

It can be a simple thought gone out of your control. A small fear, insecurity, phobia, quandary, or apprehension can seep into your mind and overpower it. If not handled properly, it can prove to be very difficult to shake off.

The habit of overthinking doesn't need special circumstances or situations to develop, but the surrounding environment can play an important role in it.

Are You an Overthinker?

To some extent, we all like to think things through. It is a good thing. Taking actions without thinking clearly or without reasonable foresight can be foolish. However, for some people, this caution takes the form of fear and leads to indecision and inaction.

Do you find yourself incapable of taking your mind of certain disturbing thoughts?

Do you feel that certain things can keep drawing your thoughts time and again towards them?

Do you fear that thinking about a few things can make you feel highly insecure, and yet you can't stop thinking about them?

Does the fear of something going wrong often leads to inaction?

Do you agree that the fear of getting up late in the morning can make you sleepless at night?

Do you start drawing far-fetched conclusions even in slightly sketchy situations?

Overthinking is a problem more common than you can think. To an extent, we all overthink. Even the most impulsive or spontaneous people around you overthink something or the other. Everyone has some hidden fears and soft spots. The problem really begins when a person starts overthinking all the time and about most of the things.

Overthinking can have disastrous effects on the life of the affected person. It can bring a person to a standstill. It can lead to strain in relationships, indecisions, inaction, and inner turmoil. It is a problem that you will need to identify and handle properly.

Defining Overthinking

If you observe closely, overthinking is a misnomer.

Thinking is a conscious process. You make a conscious decision to put your mind to something, and that process is called thinking. However, most overthinkers are simply trying to stop that process and don't have any active control over it. Yet, we like to call it overthinking.

A person would only try to stop this process when he/she knows that it isn't working in his/her favor. Unfortunately, by this time, the victim loses all the control on the thought process and feels helpless. This problem is commonly known as overthinking.

Overthinking doesn't always start as a negative process. It starts as a thought about the impact of the events that have taken place and the ways they can shape the future course of events. It is just a measure to get a head start so that you can plan better. It may be that you would like to think it through but don't want to remain engaged to that thought.

The point where you are not able to detach yourself from the thought, the problem begins. This problem is popularly known as Overthinking.

It is the point where you lose active control over your thoughts. The subconscious takes over and begins bombarding related memories, contexts, references, and hidden fears. It extrapolates.

Thinking is a mental exercise. It is a healthy game that your mind must play on a daily basis to remain healthy. It is a game it enjoys. However, this game can only be joyful as long as you have complete control.

Imagine yourself in your favorite amusement park. You get a chance to pick your favorite ride. The only catch being, you can't quit. Even the most wonderful ride in this world would become painful when you know you can't get off. It is not that the ride has gone bad. You have simply lost control over it.

This is what happens when overthinking becomes a part of life.

Types of Overthinking

Overthinking can be classified into two broad categories:

1. Ruminating: In this, the victim gets trapped in the spiral of the painful or stressful thoughts of the past and keeps reliving them. It's a trip that the victim might undertake every day, several times a day. The victim becomes forced to experience the things that are best avoided but doesn't find a way to get out of those memories. Reliving of the past can be a nightmarish experience, and if anyone is caught in it, help is very important.

2. Worrying: This is the garden variety of overthinkers. The victims are so stressed about the events to take place in the future that they hesitate in taking part in those events. Most of the problems envisioned by the victims are fictional and may never become a reality. However, the victims face problems in overcoming this fact and need help in getting out of it.

Mark Twain once said, 'I've had a lot of worries in my life, most of which never happened.'

This is true for most of the overthinkers, but they may need help in realizing this fact.

Importance of Recognizing the Problem of Overthinking

Overthinking can make the life of an affected person miserable. It is not a physical ailment, and hence the person looks fit and fine. However, the agonizing mental state of the victim can considerably affect his/her functionality.

One of the biggest problems with common issues is that they easily get ignored. We all may have it, but we never pay attention to it as we think that it is no big deal. This means that a little bit of carelessness can force a person to let this condition prevail over him/her for life. It will not only affect the victim's performance professionally but would also affect the victim's life personally.

Given below are some of the signs and symptoms of overthinking. Some signs are general, and it is easy to overlook them. However, some of these are unmistakable signs that you might be suffering from the problem of overthinking and may need help.

Remember, Overthinking is a problem but not without a solution.

Signs and Symptoms of Overthinking

Unsure of Every Decision

This is another big sign of overthinkers. They simply can't feel sure of any decision they make. Be it a simple purchase of an item in a store or a big life decision. They keep having second thoughts.

Overthinkers spend a lot of time researching those things, yet when they have made the decision, they start having doubts and second thoughts, and that makes their life miserable.

Incorrigible Habit of Reliving Embarrassing Moments in the Head

This is an unmistakable sign of overthinking.

- Overthinkersfind it difficult to let things go, especially the ones in which something bad or damaging has taken place
- They keep running negative thoughts in their head
- They are always busy trying to figure out where those things might lead them

They are trying to guess the kind of damage it would cause in their lives. They keep reliving those moments and keep feeling more and more embarrassed. They become more underconfident and scared. It puts their lives on a loop.

Incessant Mind Chatter Makes Sleeping Difficult

The mind doesn't let sleep come. The mind always keeps exaggerating the consequences of past events and the impact those things might have on their future. The mind is on a constant role play mode and becomes the dominant master.

They know that sleeping can ease the difficulty, but at that moment the sleep is the hardest thing to come by.

Overanalyze What-If Scenarios

An overthinking mind keeps analyzing several what-if scenarios. Even positive thoughts lead to negative outcomes. For instance, the mind keeps wondering what if they had said/done something positive at that point and what a great loss it has been. The regret or remorse is overwhelming.

This over analyzation of what-if scenarios can have a paralyzing effect as it impedes action.

Start Noticing Change in Tone

Overthinkers even start paying close attention to the change in tone of the people they talk to. Even if there is a slight change in the tone or behavior, they tend to associate with something they had said or done in the past. There is every possibility that the change might be there due to things happening in the personal life of the speaker, too, and even the overthinkers realize that, but they simply can't shake off the fear.

Difficulty in Forming Stable Social Bonds Due to Insecurities

Perennial insecurity is another big problem in the life of overthinkers. This makes them question almost everything repeatedly, and it doesn't work well for relationships. They are never sure about the minds of people they love, and this makes them doubtful. No one likes to get forced to prove their love every now and then.

Live in the Mind

The overthinkers are never able to enjoy the present moment as they tend to live in their minds. This habit keeps forcing them to remain in constant fear. They are never able to feel the joy of the moment fully. The baggage of past events keeps their minds occupied. They are never able to feel the joy of the moment fully.

Worry Over Things on Which They Have No Control

The mind of an overthinker is always ridden with the consciousness of things over which they have no control at all. If there is a possibility of anything going out of hand in the future, their mind would remain forever ridden with its thought. It wouldn't let them rest or sleep. Even the best of news will have no meaning or joy for them as they would keep worrying about the things which they can't control.

Inability to Accept the Grey Area

An overthinking brain likes to put things as black and white and bring as much clarity as possible. There is no scope for the grey area. Life is never as straight as black and white, and it can be really difficult to classify everything in such clear categories and this also becomes a big cause of the trouble.

Constant Fear

Constant fear of things is a permanent feature in the life of an overthinker. Such a person would always have the fear of things going wrong or people turning against him/her. This fear can make joy and trust rare commodities in life.

Muscle and Joint Pain

Overthinking also has physical symptoms, and they get manifested in the form of muscle and joint pain. There is no physical reason for such pain, but it is simply the result of excessive stress.

Headaches

Fear, insecurities, and worries make headaches a common feature in the life of an overthinker. Stress becomes a part of their lives, and they simply find it difficult to enjoy life in a carefree manner.

Fatigue

Unexplained fatigue is another common sign of overthinking. An overthinker's mind is so overtaxed that it is always aching for some relaxation. The fatigue is just another way for the body to express its desire to find some relief.

Chapter 2: Causes of Overthinking

We know overthinking is a problem. Anyone who has been through it knows that it is real mental torture. The biggest problem with overthinking is that it prolongs the agony. It makes you feel that pain in the present which may or might not come in the future. You literally create the problems for yourself, which aren't really there.

Does that mean it is a fault in the mind?

No, the root cause of overthinking is our desperation to have control. Some people really like to be in control. They want things to always go as planned. They don't like surprises. This is the reason they want to explore all the possibilities before they come face to face with them.

The human mind is complex. We casually say that our mind is not working properly, or it isn't working as per our commands; we really don't understand it.

The mind performs several crucial functions and has every function has an impact on our thinking patterns. Our intellect, emotional balance, conscious and subconscious memories, the baggage of the past, and other such things have a deep influence on the way we think.

There are several things to which we don't attach great importance, but you'll be surprised to know that even the things that you may have seen as a child and forgotten can have a deep impact on your thinking. They can become a cause of overthinking.

- *Anything you saw while walking down to your office can make you overthink*
- *The cold response of your boss after a presentation can make you overthink*
- *A simple nod from your co-worker while you expected a long reply can make you overthink*
- *Even a comparatively lighter hug from your partner can make you overthink*

There can be hundreds of triggers for overthinking. Every individual can have specific triggers. It is important to identify the things that can trigger overthinking and address them.

Most often, the things that cause overthinking are not big. They can be small and simple events, but our mind starts blowing them out of proportion. Our fears, phobias, apprehensions, and indecision can also have an important role to play in it

Some Important Causes of Overthinking are:

The Clutter in Mind

A cluttered mind is one of the biggest reasons you overthink. When the mind is full of too many unnecessary things and thinking about them at the same time, it is easy to mix things up. In such situations, overthinking is natural.

You are always afraid that you might be missing something. There is no scope of prioritization. Then you fear that you might miss something essential and this sows the seeds of fear.

A cluttered mind is also full of information that might not be relevant, but it would always try to relate you to those things, and that also leads to overthinking. You start missing the context and keep getting the references.

The Problem of Choice

We are living in the age of abundant choices. For everything, you'll find more than enough and certainly more than required alternatives, and this forces you time and again to make choices. From choosing the right shirt in the morning to wear to the office to pick up the menu for lunch, there are several important as well as useless choices that we make.

Some people are not good at this. They usually need a very long time to reach a final judgment even about smaller things. When such people are forced to make choices very frequently, it leads to overthinking.

When we are making a crucial decision, overthinking ensues, and that is natural. However, it is important to reach a final decision and to stick to it. Some people find it difficult and keep questioning their own decision. They get trapped in the vicious cycle of overthinking.

Procrastination

Inaction is another big cause of overthinking. When you keep stalling the work for the future, the fear starts to creep up in your mind. It keeps reminding you that it might not be possible to complete it on time. Your mind starts bringing up all the possibilities that might arise in case of your failure to finish the work on time. This is the birthplace of overthinking.

Once you give the control of thoughts to possibilities, there is no way to stop overthinking. This problem can be nipped in the bud if you can stop overthinking and finish the assigned tasks on time.

Too Much Social Media

Our thoughts are based on our experiences. These experiences come from our surroundings and especially from the visual stimuli. Social media plays a very big role in it as it influences our thought process greatly. The more lavishly we feed on it, the more serious the impact will be on our thinking process. Whatever is on social media is not for your taking. If you are not choosy about the things you pay attention to, it can be very hard to find a place in your mind for anything else.

When people don't exercise discretion on the intake from social media, they become a victim of the overthinking. It can make you underconfident, insecure, unhappy, and unlucky. You know that anything present on social media isn't without filters, but the mind wouldn't let this come in the way of propagating insecurities.

Expectations

High expectations can also become a cause of overthinking. Either the expectations come from you or of you, they will make you think of the probabilities, and that road surely leads to overthinking.

The expectations should be minimal, and the delivery should be maximum, and that's the only way to remain happy and content in life.

Too many expectations can burden you with results that are never in your hands. You'll find yourself compelled to somehow control or manage the outcome, and this puts you in a precarious situation. Trying to control the end is always a bad idea. It is always in our hands to put effort, but the result depends on several other factors too. It is not a good idea to put too many conditions on it.

Excessive Self-Importance

We attach too much importance to ourselves. We get identified with so many things in our life that any change starts looking like interference in our plan, and that leads to overthinking.

Even a simple change can leave us perturbed and highly disturbed. It can kick starts a new chain of thought. This chain of thought will keep on leading from one point to another, and it is very difficult to break. There is no need to do that.

In the grand scheme of things, we have a very small role to play. If we start giving ourselves too much self-importance, we may get identified to wrong things that aren't required.

If you want to stop overthinking, we need to stop building high ego-castles. Simply do the task assigned to you and stop worrying about the road where it might lead. If you do your work correctly without worrying about the result, you'll be able to put an end to the overthinking cycle.

Relationships

Relationships are the threads that keep us grounded. They tie us with each other and provide us the required support. However, they are symbiotic. They can't thrive on the effort of only one partner. Neither they can bear the load of high expectations.

When a partner starts over acknowledging his/her effort and fails to see the effort of the other partner, fissures start opening up, and they lead to overthinking. You start trying to find the reasons for all the actions and inactions. You start trying to dig meanings from actions when it is not even needed. This can be very stressful and will lead to overthinking.

Relationships need to be nurtured. You have to put in your share of effort and keep doing that without further expectations. The moment you start waiting for the other partner's share, it will lead to thoughts and then to more thoughts. This makes the mind to draw conclusions from all actions and even the inactions. It is not going to be a pleasant journey and not good at all good for your thought process as it will start calculating all the negative outcomes.

The Baggage of the Past

Our past has a deep impact on our thought process. Our intellect can't function without memories. The memories are references from the past, and hence if in the past, an action has had a negative outcome, it can affect our present thinking process. We become judgmental. We start looking at things with prejudice. We have strong barriers in our minds that can disrupt the way we may think.

The baggage of the past can be a heavy burden on our present. It may push us into inaction as we may start predicting the outcome without even moving a muscle.

This is a reason, living in the past can be dangerous for the present. If something in the past has led to negative outcomes, you must use it as a learning opportunity to find the fault in the ways of execution. Pushing all the action to a screeching halt can be dangerous.

Most people think that in this way, they can avert the wrong outcomes. However, even that doesn't happen. You can stop yourself from taking action, but you can't stop your mind. It will keep thinking about that thing either you do something or not. It will lead to overthinking and keep you focused on that very thing you want to avoid.

The best way out is to look at everything on its current merit. Don't judge it on the basis of the past.

Low Self-confidence

Our lack of self-confidence can lead to overthinking. We may start doubting everything as we do not have confidence in our abilities. In that case, we start depending a lot on luck, external forces, and failures of others. All these things are beyond our control, and hence we have no other option than to keep speculating. This gives a great fodder to our mind, which gets a free-run.

Insufficient Opportunities for Diversions

Things that are beyond our control or not to our liking keep happening all the time. If you just got reprimanded from the boss and didn't find something more engaging to do after that, the mind will get a fertile ground to graze on. It will keep on thinking about the possible outcomes of this outburst. It will extrapolate possibilities that are nowhere near the truth, but you wouldn't find them hard to believe as you are hooked to the idea that you just got reprimanded.

Think of the kids. They get scolded by their parents all the time. Soon they go to play, and their mind becomes totally focused on the game. This gives it a respite from the thought, and they escape this vicious cycle of overthinking a pass. Imagine a child who is sitting alone in a room after getting a scolding. Do you think it would be easy for that child to shake off the scolding for that child?

It is up to you to become that playful child who can shake of negative thinking patterns or the sulking child who will keep sitting in one corner brooding over the remorseful event. Intense engagement is a way to escape falling into the trap of overthinking.

Chronic Stress

Chronic stress in life also makes a person susceptible to fall into the trap of overthinking. A mind afflicted with chronic stress is already ridden with too many problems to handle, and it provides the fodder to uselessly ponder over the causes and effects. Such people start getting obsessed with the problems and keep planning ways to ditch them in the future. They seldom try to face the issues but always try to duck the problems. This gives way to the unending train of thoughts.

Negative Tendencies

Negativity begets negativity. It only happens in maths that two negatives make a positive. In real life, the more negative fodder you'll feed to your mind, the greater will be the negativity in your thoughts. Dwelling on the bad will never leave you rested.

If a person is full of negative thoughts about others, the fears of the same about the self will invariably overshadow the mind and lead to overthinking. One will have to reap what one sows.

Trauma

Bad things take place in the lives of every individual. We all have a definition of bad. What's really bad for someone may just be only an inconvenience for someone else. However, that doesn't make one person's bad less than the other.

The real problem begins when a person starts lionizing his/her bad experiences of the past and starts living in a cocoon. This cocoon may seem to provide protection, but it is fragile and porous. It doesn't stop the insecurities from penetrating the protective shell. The fears can keep traumatizing the victim. They always keep the victim in a state of high alert. They may the victim think the bad things over and over again.

The longer you resist facing your fears, the stronger they will get. They will keep weighing you down. There can be no escape from this experience if you don't brace yourself up and face it once and for all. The fear of facing the trauma of the past will only lead to overthinking about it.

You would start planning several steps ahead to avoid such things in totality. However, you can have no active control over the results of each and every action that you perform. Whenever any outcome is outside your planned structure, it will lead to detailed planning ahead. You leave no scope for impromptu improvisations. This can be damaging for you on the whole.

Overthinking can be triggered by many things, and these are just some of the things that lead to overthinking. Most people start blaming their minds for excessively thinking things or remaining engaged to a particular thought for too long. They simply want their minds to stop thinking.

This is a big problem.

Your mind is not the source of the problem. The mind will always work on the fodder you provide it. You can choose to keep engaged in a productive manner or offer opportunities for self-destruction, but you can't bring it to a standstill. The ability to continuously have thoughts is something that the mind has developed over thousands of years of evolution. It is the same in you as that of a peaceful man. The problem is not with the mind but the way we are using it and the fodder we are providing to the mind.

If you want your mind to be at peace, the first thing that you need to watch is the kind of information that is getting in. When your mind is receiving information without filters, there is every possibility of having mental diarrhea.

Chapter 3: Information Overload- A Latent Threat

The most dangerous threats are those that can't be seen

Information is a privilege. Before the 15th Century, the information traveled at a very slow pace. In this period, the printing press was invented, and people got a new medium to get information. It was still very slow and limited in reach, but it was a slow and steady step in the right direction of education and awareness.

5 centuries later, today, we live in the age of the internet. Today, the data can travel even faster than the speed of light. It can penetrate the farthest reaches. However, in the pursuit of making it more and more accessible, it is now very freely available and hence has started becoming a problem for our minds.

We live in an age where anything big happening anywhere in the world can reach us instantly wherever we are, irrespective of our condition or preparation to grasp it, and this has turned into a problem.

The Ways in Which Information Overload is Affecting Our Minds

Information is power. However, what do you do with unlimited power for which you have no use or application? Even that power stays with you and occupies space. All kinds of information occupy space in our minds and keep getting registered in our memory. The information that we can't use remains stored as clutter, and this clutter also keeps the mind engaged.

Case 1

You receive the tragic news of a bomb blast that happened at some remote corner of the world. The most humane reaction to this news is remorse. You can't do anything about it, but as a human being, you'll feel sorry. This is natural and genuine.

The problem is that it wouldn't stop here.

That information will keep coming back to you in various forms from various information sources. We call them social media platforms. They will just not stop at informing you; they'll try to engage you. They'll try to invoke a deeper emotion at your end. Every campaign would have a different motive. You may not have anything to do with them, but you can't stop getting affected.

That single incident of a bomb blast will boomerang to you from several sources and start affecting your psyche. It can push you into thinking that the world has become very insecure all of a sudden. It is not the information that's coming to you now but the opinions of the various sources which want to prove their points.

This information can become potent enough to push you into thinking that the world has become so insecure and violent.

Remember, we are still talking about that same bomb blast. But, by now, you may have heard about it dozens of times from dozens of different sources.

You are not the only one being fed this news. Even your friend circle is also being fed the same news. This can also become a topic of conversation at the bar table while you have a few drinks with your friends. Now, imagine hearing the same things from the mouth of the people you know. It will have a much deeper impact on your brain. It will start getting registered in the deeper parts of your brain.

When you feel insecure, it is good for the market. An insecure person is more likely to spend as the future never looks like a very secure idea. Shopping also helps as a stress reliever. It also provides the required diversion to many, and the market knows it. You invariably become a product.

Case 2

You receive a notification of a social media platform about a friend on vacation. It is a nice and beautiful picture. You could like it or turn off the screen of the phone, and this would come to an end. But, more than 90% of the people are not able to resist the temptation to look further.

You want to put the phone away and get back to what you were doing originally. However, the chances of that happening have gone down considerably now. From one picture to another and then to other references, social media has the power to transport you into another world. It will promise you a closer look into the lives of others and then reflect on the futility of your own.

Just a few minutes ago, you were sitting content busy doing something useful. The next thought that comes to your mind is the amount of time it has been for you since you took such a vacation. Your mind starts doing cost calculations and tries to find the viability of the plan. Then it would also think about the joy, happiness, and contentment in the life of others and remind you of the void that you must feel. Remember, it is not important that you ever felt it before or not. This is the age of comparative analysis.

A simple post can trick you into planning your own trip and will make you feel the things that lack in your life. It is not important that you needed them originally or not.

This is the kind of damage excessive information can do in your life.

In both cases, you'll see that the unavailability of information wouldn't have made any difference in your life. Even controlled inlet of information wouldn't have mattered much. But, you get an unhindered excess without use and training to handle that information, and it can bring havoc, disturbance, and disillusionment in your life.

Social media has become very powerful. It is getting more and more technologically advanced. The marketers are getting highly equipped with the tools to judge your mood, likings, and actions. Every piece of information that you come across will have an impact on your mind. You can't avoid it. The more information you receive, the more fodder you will provide to your mind. This can kickstart a process of useless gossip-mongering as what starts as innocent pondering over thoughts can turn into overthinking. It will have the binding elements of fears, insecurities, aspirations, and apprehensions.

In this day and age, consider yourself a participant in a very large buffet. There can be hundreds of things to eat. You pay once for the entry. That makes you eligible to eat as much as you can and as many things as you like.

You have already paid for it, and hence no one can question your tasting a little bit of everything. But, your digestion system is definitely not going to like it. It is going to get confused with all the wide varieties of food items at your disposal. There is no way for you to know the things that can be allergic to you. Hence, you also stand the risk of getting allergic reactions and infections.

The best way out is to feed on limited things that are good for your health and the gut. Greed to get more and more will only land you in deeper troubles. This is the lesson we need to remember while we are on social media platforms.

The more we feed on unsolicited information, the higher is the possibility of the mind getting on the track of overthinking. Most of our fears and resentments come from the comparisons we make with others. We are less concerned about what we have made with our lives and more about where others have reached. We fail to understand that we only see the things which are being projected to us using several filters. Even they might be battling with even more serious issues in their respective lives. However, the mind can easily side-track this and make you think about your failures time and again.

Information overload is happening from all the corners. However, I brought up social media platforms here as they have a direct and deep impact on our lives. The information that we get from TV channels, newspapers, magazines also affects us, but most of us are able to recover from it easily. The hangover of the information received from social media platforms is long-lasting and severe.

Today, an average American handles at least 5 times more information than what was handled in 1986. All sources estimated that around 30 exabytes of information existed till the end of the 20th century or less than two decades ago. We have created more than 300 exabytes of information in the last decade itself. Around 500 hours of videos are uploaded on YouTube every minute. This means that in an hour, more than 30,000 hours of videos are uploaded on the website. This is just one video streaming website. There are a countless number of such websites that are serving content to you. Most of the content present on these websites may be entertaining or informative but can not be relevant to your field of interest. Giving all such information storage space in your mind is simply going to create more clutter.

Overcoming information overload is not an easy task in this age of the internet. Information is being sprayed upon you from all the directions. You become a receptor of information either you like it or not most of the time. However, it is still in your control to choose to keep all that information of not.

Ways to Overcome Information Overload

Limit the Distractions

The number of sources from which we can be getting information can be unlimited these days. Even the streets have screens bigger than homes displaying all sorts of information. You mostly can't control the kind of news that comes on TV. Neither you can control the rambling of the radio jockeys you listen to while driving. However, you can still control a lot of information that gets delivered to you personally.

Our computers and smartphones can be the storehouse of unsolicited information. Smartphones can have multitudes of applications that might boast of connecting you to the whole universe.

The important question to ask here is, do you really wish that?

Get rid of social media applications and other such platforms that add no value to your life. These are the tools to deprive you of your personal time. They don't allow even a minute of me-time as you are always longing to check the status of others.

The lower the number of such applications, the lesser the information overload in your life.

Also, separate email accounts for important work as miscellaneous work. No matter how hard you try to categorize the marketing email campaigns in your inbox, they do find ways to sneak into your main inbox to clutter your mind.

Minimize the Decision Fatigue

Decision fatigue has become a real problem of this age. There was a time when even the departmental stores had limited inventory, and you could easily find the things you were looking for. Shopping was easy, and the main problem used to be the money to buy the things you needed. The money is still a problem for many but besides that what to buy in the available money has emerged as a bigger problem.

As per marketwatch.com, average grocery stores in the US had around 7000 products in their inventory, even in the 1990s. The number of inventory items has increased to 40000-50000 now. This means you now have to choose from thousands of new products. Before you can pick the things you need, you may have to reject or ignore dozens more.

Many people are unaware that even the simple task of choosing the shirt to wear in the morning requires a considerable amount of decision making. The same goes for choosing the items for lunch or dinner, and these are the things which really don't matter to you. Think of the impact things that matter would have on your life. You may spend hours and hours thinking about those things and would keep making plans subconsciously. This is the stepping stone towards the overthinking pit.

Overthinkers can spend countless amounts of time trying to figure out the right things to buy. Even after making the purchase, they can keep having second thoughts. This keeps happening to them time and again in almost everything that requires decision making.

When you are forced to make decisions from morning to evening in everything in your life, the mind is never fresh to make important decisions. This is a reason most successful people try to keep themselves free from such constraints. Have you ever wondered why Mark Zuckerberg, the CEO of Facebook, wears the same t-shirt every day or why even the President of the USA appears in the same suit daily?

These are the leaders entrusted with the responsibility of making important decisions in their life. But, even the smaller decisions would also affect their lives in a similar fashion. To avoid getting drained by the decision fatigue, they made a wise choice of avoiding decision fatigue in life.

They removed the need for making decisions in the areas which didn't require much attention. This is a better way to avoid decision fatigue in life and reduce the information overload on the mind.

Give Yourself a Break

It is important that you keep taking frequent breaks within your workday. A few minutes of break to reboot after an hour of work is not a very bad idea. Don't do anything during this time. Don't talk to your co-workers or do anything else. Simply take a few deep breaths and give your mind a few minutes of break. You can also take small power naps in these breaks. If you like, walk around a bit to give your libs a bit of stretching.

The purpose of this break should be to give your mind a small recess from the current process of intensive thinking. If you think it will weaken your focus, then you are wrong; in fact, these breaks can make your focus and clarity even better. These breaks will also help your mind in getting used to active diversions whenever needed.

Lower the Burden on Mind

We come across several pieces of information in our day to day lives that may look important. Most of the time, we keep mulling over those ideas subconsciously. We pay very little attention to those ideas; however, this doesn't mean that those things don't affect the processing of your mind. A section of your brain keeps those ideas stored and keeps working on them in the background. This all happens because you didn't relieve your mind from the burden of those things.

The best way to deal with this issue is to make notes of such things when they come into your mind. If you are not going to use them in the near future, there is no use keeping your mind busy with them. This simple act will help you in lowering the burden of new information on your mind.

If there is any piece of information you liked and may like to use it in the future, simply write it down on a notepad or make a note on your smartphone or register is somewhere else you like. Don't let it simply linger in your mind as a strange idea. It is a great way to keep your brain free to do its regular tasks.

Don't Multitask

Another big problem of this age is the fashion of taking pride in being a multi-tasker. A person can have a dynamic personality and diverse knowledge, and that would be an asset. But a person who can do several things at the same time can't be doing anything good with dedication.

The people who are multitasking are usually doing too many unimportant things at the same time. Their focus is broken, and their mind is occupied with several things at the same time. This would mean that they would be using the mind at its full capacity. This might be useful in stressful situations where it is a question of survival, but exerting so much pressure on the mind even in normal circumstances would only lead to overtaxing and it is not beneficial in any way.

It is correct that our mind is capable of doing some magnificent things. It is powerful and is at work constantly. On average, our minds can have around 50,000 thoughts and perform several functions at the same time. But, when people consider these figures, they don't take into account the number of activities our mind is performing in the background. It also has the responsibility of running the complex machinery called our body. Most of the functions in the body are also controlled by the mind. It also deals with all the memories, the conscious ones, as well as the subconscious ones. When you tax your mind too much, you are unknowingly putting too much pressure on it.

Overloading the mind is not a good practice, and it should be avoided as far as possible.

Information overload is a latent threat to the mind. The amount of pressure it exerts on your conscious memory is nothing as compared to the impact it has on the subconscious one. The same thoughts can keep circling in your mind even when you don't think of them. The best way to deal with the issue is to lower the information overload on the mind and keep it as much relaxed as possible.

Once you put your mind into the practice of engaging in multiple tasks at the same time, you would find it really difficult to focus on a single task when needed. Your mind would keep wandering here and there, and that can be a very frustrating experience.

Chapter 4: Negative Effects of Overthinking

Overthinking can be really taxing not only for your mind but also for your body. The mind is the control unit of the body, and if it is feeling the pressure, the whole body can't escape reeling under the pressure.

Overthinking has a profound impact on your body, mind, and emotions. Not only does it affect you mentally and emotionally, but it also leads to deep cognitive impairment. For a very long time, overthinking remained an ignored problem. No one paid much attention to it for a very long time. However, the stats now tell a very chilling tale of the extent to which it affects the people in general. The Anxiety and Depression Association of American says that around 40 million adults in the US suffer from anxiety disorders. This is the most common mental illness in the US. It is a highly treatable condition, yet only 36.9% of the patients suffering from it actually come for treatment.

Anxiety disorder is the broader category, and a number of problems like panic disorder, social anxiety disorder, various phobias, obsessive-compulsive disorders, posttraumatic stress disorder, and persistent depressive disorders come under this condition.

Overthinking in itself is not a disease, but it can be a precursor to many mental illnesses. If left ignored, overthinking could become a very big problem for the victim as it can impede the normal life of the victim.

Living with an overthinking brain is like living in a high seismic area in an unstable building. It will always have a high probability of collapsing, and the fear of collapse would never go away.

It may not have a significant impact on your physical appearance, but internally you never be able to be in peace.

Physical Effects

Energy Drain

Overthinking can make you feel tired and lethargic. This is a common sign felt by most people struggling with the issue of overthinking. Most people experience the feeling of energy drain and lethargy due to mental fatigue. They feel that it is simply because they are fed up of thinking a lot. However, it is much deeper than that.

When you are ruminating a lot, your brain rapidly goes through a lot of possibilities, and most of them are bad. This is the nature of the mind to look at the worst-case scenarios. This invokes a stress response in the body. The body starts releasing cortisol, the main stress hormone in the body. This hormone is very effective in many things. It can raise your blood pressure, make your vessels contract and expand rapidly. It can get you worked up in a jiffy. The objective of this hormone is to supply you with the adrenaline rush in a split second so that you can escape any stress scenario. But, because only your mind is doing all the work and not the body, all that rush simply settles down and then comes the relaxation effect in the form of lethargy. You might have experienced a brief period of complete nullness moments after extreme stress has passed over, that's the moment. This is the reason you can start feeling energy drained and lethargic due to overthinking.

Change in Appetite

Overthinking can lead to loss of appetite. When there is too much cortisol in your body, it can signal the hypothalamus in the brain to focus all the energy at one point, and hence you may not feel things like hunger, fatigue, and sleep. The hunger hormone ghrelin gets released by the body periodically, and it is not regulated by the amount of food you have in your gut but by hormonal release and time. The stress hormone can even signal your body to focus completely on survival and the body can also survive on the stored energy for long.

However, in the case of chronic stress caused by habitual overthinking, the stress hormone can even increase your appetite a lot. There are certain comfort foods like sweets or high carb foods that lead to the release of neurotransmitters like dopamine and serotonin that may make you feel happy and help in case of low mood. You may want to keep hogging on these things as they would start providing you the required relief.

Insomnia

Sleep is a relaxed state of the body. In order to sleep, your body needs to be in a completely relaxed state. Stress and anxiety keep your body aroused. Your blood pressure and heart rate remain up, and you may find it really difficult to sleep. To make matters worse, your brain would still be overthinking a lot of things making sleep even more difficult.

A big problem with sleep disorders caused by overthinking is that it begins a chain of cause and effect. First, you are unable to sleep due to stress, and then you get more stress as you are not able to sleep properly, and your body isn't rested enough. If the overthinking problem isn't tackled on time, it can lead to sleep disorders and insomnia pretty quickly.

Mental Effects

Mental Rut

The mental rut is an agonizing loop. You get stuck in a negative spiral that simply keeps dragging the victim down the rabbit hole of negative thinking. All the thoughts that the victim has are about avoiding negative outcomes, but they don't lead to any kind of positive door. All the energy goes into avoiding the problems while the problems still stand there in the face. Simply getting through the day becomes a struggle for the victim.

The victim simply chooses to live in constant denial mode. Not accepting the circumstances will never change them. It will only make the victim more defenseless.

It seems like a very uncommon phenomenon, but you'd be surprised to know that most overthinkers are the victims of this mental rut. They are unable to find a way out as they don't even try.

Cognitive Impairment

Cognitive impairment is another risk that most overthinkers face. Excessive overthinking affects the functioning of the mind. The mind becomes more insecure and defensive.

Risk of Mental Illnesses

Mental illnesses are very common in overthinkers as their reliance on their minds increases a lot. However, in the process, they don't allow their minds to function at its full capacity. The mind simply remains tied to certain insecurities and starts forming the world around them.

Loss of Problem-Solving Skills

Loss of problem-solving skills is another issue such people face as their complete focus is not on solving the problem but avoiding it completely. They are simply trying to find an escape route. However, you can run from anything, but you're the shackles you have created in your own mind.

Memory Issues

Excessive stress caused by overthinking negative things can lead to memory issues and emotional problems. The victim starts attaching emotions to even logical tasks, and that compromises their judgments. The mind is so focused on some negative things that it starts ignoring any other issue, and that leads to memory problems too.

Emotional Effects

Fear and Anxiety

The amygdala is the fear center of the brain. It is the area of the brain responsible for evoking fear and anxiety. When you overthink a lot, this area becomes dominant in its function and keeps you feeling fearful. There may not be any real reason to fear, but when you are fearful, your actions become more reserved, and hence the mind feels that you are less likely to take actions that might invoke an aggressive response. Therefore, the amygdala keeps increasing the stress and fear response in the mind.

Inaction

The action would lead to a reaction, and then the mind would again have to strategize for a response. In overthinkers, this system works on a whole new level. An overthinking mind keeps making strategies and then extrapolates them. It doesn't lead to any real action, as that would lead to a practical reaction that can be beyond the control of the victim. Hence, the mind keeps the victim in a virtual world where the strategies are being tested to find the right approach. However, on the ground, nothing gets done. Overthinkers simply keep thinking, they keep putting things for tomorrow as they want to avoid uncertain or unlikely outcomes but that just leads to complete inaction.

Effects on the Brain Function

Impact on Neuroplasticity

Neuroplasticity is a magnificent process through which the brain cells keep renewing themselves. This process goes on forever. This is the reason earlier the older folks in the tribe were called the wise men. They had more experience, and although their bodies would become weak, their brains would remain fully functional. They would have more experience in their hand, and hence they were fit to advise.

Overthinking leads to excessive stress, which has a negative effect on the regeneration of new brain cells. It can slow the process of regeneration greatly. in fact, the brain can convert a chemical called Glutamate into a neurotoxin that can start killing the brain cells. It starts creating free radicals in the brain that create holes in the brain cell walls. Insomnia, alcohol addiction, and substance abuse are some of the problems that can originate due to this problem.

Neurodegenerative Disorders

Neurodegenerative disorders are those in which the brain cells slowly start losing their structure. It has been medically proven by science that too much cortisol production can interfere with the generation of new neurons or the brain cells, it will ultimately lead to the shrinking of the brain. The brain would also start losing its capacity to remember things and function properly. Dementia is one of the most common types of neurodegenerative disorders that can take place due to constant rumination and worrying.

Chapter 5: Controlling the Mind

Overthinking is a complex problem, but the solution to this problem is simple. To overthinking, you only need to stop thinking about negative things. Most people are fearful of the whole process of thinking. They find their minds in such a turmoil that they want to put a stop to the constant chatter in their heads. Fortunately, that's neither required nor possible.

One can only put a stop on the thoughts in your mind when it stops working completely, and by then, most definitely, even the person in question would also cease to exist.

A thinking brain is a good thing. An overthinking brain is even a better thing. We call people with such minds as geniuses. The problem begins when the mind starts to overthink negative things or the things we are not very pleased to ponder.

There is a possibility for the mind to think in the right direction or the wrong direction. Unfortunately, the mind chooses the wrong course, and that leads to all the problems. The solution to this problem doesn't lie in bringing the mind of a complete stop altogether. You simply need to train the mind to change its course and think in the right direction.

Before you start working on the solution, it is very important that you clearly understand the problem. Running in the wrong direction very fast wouldn't take you in the right direction. You will ultimately have to change your course of action.

The process will be slow, and you will have to be persistent. The mind can be very resilient. It will wield more control. But, in the end, if you show some perseverance, this problem can be corrected.

There are several ways to do this. From techniques to corrections, this book will cover all the aspects of getting over the problem of overthinking.

The first step in the right direction is to learn to control the mind. You will have to make some fundamental changes in your thinking so that you can come out of the cycle of fear and anxiety.

Overcome Mental Clutter

Decluttering of mind is essential if you want your mind to think in a positive manner. A mind cluttered with a thousand things will keep providing negative fodder. You may dispel one, though, and before it has disappeared, the new one will arise like zombies.

Mental clutter also makes you feel tied to things. You carry an unknown burden, and you don't know its worth.

For once, sit down and tabulate the things or thoughts that cause the trouble. Facing them is the only way to form a strategy to quell them.

Sorting the mental clutter is an important part of understanding the things that are causing the trouble. You must understand that it is not your mind that's causing the mischief. The mind is simply an amplifier. It will simply play the things that you put inside it. If you'll keep useless things ready to be fed into the machine, the product would never be as per your desire.

Putting the house in order is imperative. Every thought in the mind cannot be important, and neither all the thoughts can be scary. However, if you don't know the exact number of scary ones, you'll fear everything.

Cut the mental clutter and find the things that you find really disturbing. Whatever is of no consequence should be pushed into oblivion. All your fears and insecurities should be clear in front of you.

Cultivating Optimism Through Positive Responses to Repetitive Thoughts

Fear and anxiety work as the fuel of negativity. The more you fear, the darker it will get. You can't fight fear with anger. Two negatives don't make a positive. The only way to invoke positivity is to cultivate optimism.

If you have failed twice at something and faced public humiliation, your mind would try its best to convince you to not to try ever. It may start running all the humiliating moments in a loop. This can be disempowering.

The mind tries to convince you that you are not good enough at the thing you are trying to do.

Aggression, frustration, anger, or flight cannot be the answers. Your response should be that you are good enough, and you can do even better. This was not your best attempt.

There is a beautiful quote,

Failure is not the end of your story,

It is the beginning of your comeback story.........

In every aspect of life, your response to every stressful thought should be positive. This positivity would bring your confidence and charm back. It will help you in winning yourself back from your mind.

Negativity can push you in the dark corners of self-pity. You may have thoughts of self-rejection. You may feel that no one loves you or cares for you.

The fact is, even if you can't love yourself, how can you expect others to do the same. Love yourself. You know the positive aspects of your own personality. Explore them.

To fight extreme darkness, you don't need floodlights. Even a simple spark is enough to shake the empire of darkness. Always remember that darkness is fragile. It may look complete and overwhelming, but even a small spark of light can put a hole in it.

You don't need to find a whole lot to get over this blanket of negative thought cycle. Start with finding one thing that makes you lovable, and I'm sure that you'll be able to find many. You'll see that fighting the dark isn't that very difficult.

Cultivating optimism in your thinking is a winning strategy you will need to adopt.

Think Something New

There are some comments to which we have no comeback. The mind tries to lead us into things from which we can't recover. You may not find enough optimism to get over it.

So, do you surrender?

But, why do you need to play on the terms of the mind? Sometimes it's just better to sit and relax.

Diversion from a negative thought is the best way to avoid getting caught in the negative thought processes. If your mind is dragging you towards some really depressing things, try thinking of something completely different.

Think of something that really brings a smile on your lips. Engage in an activity that's completely absorbing.

This might look difficult at the moment. But, believe me, it is an easy thing to do. It just requires some practice and determination to break the unending loop of thoughts.

Find things that are powerful enough to distract you from negativity. It can be a hobby, your favorite pet, anything else you like to think about, simply think about those things when your mind starts racing towards negativity, and you'll find it easy to break the chain of thoughts.

Learn to Live in the Moment

One of the biggest problems of this age is that we have started to live in an autopilot mode. Most of the things that we do are habitual. When you do things out of habit, much thought is not required. You can still go on with that act while your mind is busy scheming something else.

This means the mind gets a lot of free time. There is a great amount of time when you are not using the mind actively. This is the time; the brain starts toying with thoughts.

We have made lives too easy and comfortable for ourselves. We also don't like to face too many challenges in conducting the day to day chores in our lives, and that helps in keeping the mind in the autopilot mode.

We weren't always like this. For our ancestors, the clear focus was a necessity. Lack of focus could get them killed. Nowadays, there are very few things that require such undivided attention.

Even while you are driving a car on a road full of traffic, you are doing a dozen things. You are listening to music on the stereo; you may even talk to a friend sitting beside you. You keep looking outside but not necessarily to navigate the traffic but to find something of interest. All this while, the mind can still be busy thinking about something that happened a week ago in the office and the response that should have suited the situation but didn't come from you.

All this is possible because we have got used to this mindless act of being in an autopilot mode. We forget that we are essentially a thriving life that was never meant to live the life of a robot.

We seldom pay attention to the things we do and say at that moment. Our mind does all the accounting later on and then reprimands us. The seed of overthinking gets sowed due to our overdependence on this habitual functioning lifestyle.

The moment you start living mindfully and pay proper attention to the things at that very moment, the cycle of overthinking that thing, later on, would come to an end as you will conclude the affairs at that moment, and hence there will be no residual karma.

Mindful living is a good way to break the cycle of overthinking. It gives you better control of the mind, and you are able to think more clearly and judiciously.

Understanding the Importance of Perspective

Most of the overthinking process is a result of wrong identification. We feel identified to certain things in life, and that puts us in compartments. We begin comparisons from there and start computing the futility of our lives.

From the early days of upbringing, we are taught to have goals. We set life goals and then further subdivide them into milestones. A thing created for our convenience ultimately becomes our destiny. We remain nothing more than those goals. Our hopes, aspirations, joys, and deepest, darkest fears are attached to those goals. This is a big cause of the problem.

We set smaller goals for ourselves and then become too rigid on them. Smaller goals also mean that our perspective gets narrow. We find ourselves unable to see the grand scheme of things. When someone else tries to do something like that, we call that person a lunatic.

If you don't want some thoughts to completely overpower you, widen your perspective. Don't feel identified with smaller or inconsequential things that are limited just to you. Think wider, and you'll find that thinking about your problems wouldn't remain a problem. It is a good way to evolve out of the problem of overthinking.

Learning to Deal with Uncertainties

All things said and done; there is no way to eliminate all the uncertainties in this world. In fact, even this big blue earth is not immune to uncertainties. The creation of this world is a result of such uncertainties.

When we do something, there is no way to control the effect. At best, you can speculate the effect. There are always several external factors at play. However, when you have accepted the fact that there can be uncertainties on the way, dealing with them becomes easy. It isn't that the uncertainties go soft on you, simply you become more open to change.

Learn to live with it. There is no other way to survive.

Letting the Future Be

This is just the continuation of the point above. When you accept the fact that the result can be different from what you expect, it becomes easier to let the future be. You don't try to change anything and adapt.

You come out of the logical fallacy of grandfather paradox. Things in this world can exist independently. The cause of effect at one time may look significant, but it may not be detrimental in reality.

The best thing is to simply let the future be. Don't try to alter it as per your design. Adaptation is the right way to survive. There is no way that we could have come this far, changing everything as per our whims and fancies.

Don't Procrastinate Indefinitely

Overthinkers have a tendency to leave things for later. Their mind is testing things virtually, and hence they don't deem any physical action necessary. However, the longer you take to make a move, the stronger the grip of overthinking would become. If you really want to stop overthinking, learn to take action immediately. If you think that you'll give your mind the time of a day to get ready to take action and it would agree, you are wrong. It will find ways to convince you to not act.

The best way out is to take action as soon as possible. Action will lead to cause and effect, and you will need to respond, and hence you'll get past the stage of overthinking it in the mind.

Chapter 6: Getting Over Anxiety and Panic-Beating Overthinking at Its Best

The most common effect of overthinking is anxiety. It is a state of restlessness, fear, and angst that trips off the victim completely. A normally working person can start behaving in an uneasy fashion. It begins with slight discomfort and, if left unchecked, can mature to panic attacks.

The Signs of Anxiety are:

- You feel your heart beating at an unusually fast pace
- Your breathing becomes rapid
- You experience light headedness
- You can feel the butterflies in your gut
- You start feeling visibly agitated
- You start having irrational fears
- It would impossible for you to focus on a particular thing other than the thing you are worried about
- You might even feel your muscles getting tense
- There is a sudden restlessness inside you

- There is something inside you that wants to avoid the things expected to happen

If you have felt these emotions, then you fully well understand what anxiety is and the kind of impact it has on the mind. Anxiety isn't a diagnosable condition. You simply feel its presence inside you.

Various things like your brain chemistry, environment, and genetics can contribute to the development of anxiety. However, your mental state will remain the leading contributor to the existence of the condition.

Three Brain Areas Playing a Key Role in Causing Stress and Anxiety

Amygdala: It is an almond-shaped area in the center of the brain that's responsible for invoking feelings of fearing and anxiety. This part plays a key role in the processing of emotions, and when you are feeling highly stressed, it invokes fear and anxiety as a protective mechanism. It senses the threats and alerts the brain to signs of danger. This is the part of the brain that responds to various anxiety triggers. For instance, if a person had ever had a drowning accident, this part of the brain would keep invoking the fear of drowning whenever the victim goes near a water body. The whole exercise is for saving the victim from drowning ever, but it is an escapist approach. The trigger can be any unpleasant episode registered in the memory of the victim.

Hippocampus: It is a complex brain structure that is embedded deep into the temporal lobe. This part of the brain is responsible for recording memories of all sorts, short-term as well as long-term memories. Memories of traumatic and life-threatening events, as well as unpleasant memories, are stored in this part of the brain. Problems in this area can lead to various mental disorders. Excessive stress and childhood trauma can cause shrinking of this part of the brain, which can further complicate the issues.

Hypothalamus: This is a very busy area of the brain. It acts as the command center. It listens to various signals sent by the body in forms of hormones and chemical signals. It then communicates these signals in forms of hunger, satiety, fear, pain, etc. The fight or flight response felt during anxiety is created by this part of the brain.

There can be various triggers that lead to anxiety. A trigger is external stimuli that your brain receives through various senses. It brings back memories of the past traumatic events, and various sections of the brain get on to work to create the flight or fight response.

Every individual can have different triggers for anxiety. There can be events, situations, people, or things that trigger anxiety.

Common Triggering Events:

- Watching someone in agonizing pain, anger or a state of fear
- Looking at someone resembling a tormentor in the past or having similar traits
- A place with links to any traumatic incident
- Any smell that reminds of you of the traumatic incident

Anxiety can have a paralyzing effect. The brain simply becomes defenseless. Escape starts looking like the best resort at that moment.

Anxiety disorder is one of the most common mental problems that Americans face. There are more than 40 million people currently suffering from anxiety disorders of various types. It is a highly treatable condition, but most people are never able to recover from it as they never seek help.

As explained above, if left unaddressed, excessive stress and anxiety can affect the functioning of the brain. It can shrink various portions of the brain and impair memory and other cognitive abilities.

Anxiety can impair the normal functioning of a person as an unknown fear stays with the victim forever. Uncertainty becomes a part of life, and people start shying away from unbridled public exposure.

Most things that lead to anxiety are not real threats. It is the mind trying to put you into a protective cocoon. There are several ways to counter stress and anxiety effectively.

Ways to Deal with Anxiety

Mindfulness

Mindfulness is the phenomenal concept to help one remain grounded in the present. We all like to believe that we live in the present, but that's not correct. We live in a world identified with several things and memories to back that up.

For instance, if you are a successful person, you may expect people to greet you when they meet you. It is because you are identified with your position and feel that it commands that respect. When someone whom you expect doesn't greet, it kickstarts the thought process about the significance of that event. Normally, the greeting might not have meant anything to you. But, because you feel so identified with your position that the absence of greeting might begin to look like a question to your authority. Thoughts and memories also have a profound role to play in this whole mash-up.

This event would keep running in your mind long after you have left that place. It doesn't remain a simple question of not greeting you anymore. It may also start creating self-doubt, and you may begin questioning your relevance and standing.

All this happens because the whole process is running in the mind. Very little is being said or expressed. The mind is simply interpreting the events as per its current state and conditioning.

The more you get identified with things in this world, the greater will be the flow of thoughts. We start living in those virtual identities. Our identifications create attachments to certain ideas, and that leads to all this friction. The more we feel identified with certain things in life, the greater will be our sense of judgment as we start creating specifications. There will be rigidity and dogma. Our perspective will get limited. There will be no acceptability in our attitude as we stop looking at things as they are because we want to see them as per our beliefs.

Mindfulness is the art of living in the present. It helps you in looking at the things as they are without the glass of judgment. You don't form preconceived notions about things. You remain open to new things. This makes you flexible and reduces the chances of friction.

5 Basic Principles of Mindfulness

Detachment: It is a way of living that helps you in remaining detached. To live in this world and enjoy it, you don't need to feel identified with it. There is no need to categorize things as good and bad. The way we look at things can change the way they behave for us.

Once two professors were walking on the grounds of their university. One looked at the lackluster winter afternoon with the Sun not shining brightly and felt that it was such a dull day. The other professor was blind, and hence he couldn't see the Sun, but we could feel the warmth of the Sun on his shoulders and felt it was such a wonderful day. Both of them were at the same place but weren't looking at the Sun with the same perspective.

When we get too much identified with things, we start judging them based on our past experiences and not on their merit. There is always an addition and subtraction. You have fixed reference points. You keep reliving those past experiences and memories. The problem with memories is that they are a thing of the past. If they are good, you can't have them now, and they'll always keep ruining your current experience with the comparison.

In a detached way of living, you simply judge things on the way, you experience them at that moment. You don't qualify them on your past experiences. This makes every experience unique. It can increase the joy in life and give you a greater chance of feeling contentment.

Non-judgmental Attitude: The biggest reason for our unhappiness is our judgmental attitude. We judge everything on the basis of our past experiences. We label everything and then make firm beliefs about things that can make us happy and sad. These classifications have little to do with the way that things really turn out to be. Mindfulness is all about experiencing things as they are without judging them on the basis of old ideas.

Living in the Present: Most people never let the past go. They hold on to the past very strongly. Due to this, they are never able to enjoy their present. They keep working hard to make their future like their past, even better than it. However, they miss the present. Almost all of us fall into this category. We spend all our lives working towards our retirement, knowing fully well that there is no surety that we'll be there to enjoy it or the things we are doing would matter then. It is important that every moment that you spend is memorable and meaningful. Live to enjoy every moment of life.

Acceptance: We have become very rigid in our beliefs. We resent any kind of deviation. Most people are never even able to accept themselves as they are. They are always in a constant pursuit to change themselves for an image that looks better. This attitude only brings unhappiness and discontentment. When you try to go against nature without reason, the results are never very pleasant. Mindfulness helps you in accepting everything as it is. Working for betterment is something entirely different, but loathing something cannot be a part of the plan as it would lead to stress and anxiety.

Openness: Mindfulness is the idea of letting go of rigid ideas and opening up to new things and experiences. You don't stick to certain belief systems because you have been taught about it or have seen people follow them. You remain open to new experiences.

Mindfulness is a very simple practice as it requires you to do very little. You don't have to carry any baggage. You just remain conscious of the things as they happen. When you walk, you just don't move your legs that lead to displacement, you experience the movement and feel it. When you eat something, you don't judge the food on the basis of the taste it should have. You feel the taste every time you eat it. You pay close attention to every aspect of life.

Because it is such a simple way of living life, most people find it very difficult. It is a powerful practice that you follow in each and everything you do in life. This is the thing that makes it difficult as we are used to doing things on an autopilot mode or mindlessly.

However, practicing mindfulness can help you in leaving the baggage of the past. You stop judging things on the basis of preconceived notions. You become conscious of every breath you take and start enjoying every moment as it comes. You don't label things. You stop attaching too much importance to things as they are.

This practice can decrease stress, anxiety, depression, fatigue, irritability, and emotional reactivity. It can put a stop to constant rumination as it enables you to keep the mind open. When you stop judging things on past experiences, there is less scope for anxiety originating from emotional triggers.

Purposeful attention becomes an important part of your life. You don't let things pass by without experiencing them on merit. You become more focused and attentive.

If you want to lower stress and anxiety in life, practicing mindfulness can give you a good ground, to begin with.

Visualization

Visualization is a great way to lower stress and anxiety. The main cause of anxiety is excessive focus on some negative emotions. It simply remains hooked on to negativity and doesn't allow you to come out of it. One major problem here is that there are so many negative emotions that they don't allow positive thoughts to come to your mind.

Visualization can be a big asset in such scenarios. It is a simple practice of visualizing something sweet and pleasant that you have always wished for but don't relate to it strongly. It detaches you from the negative emotions and gives your mind the required diversion.

You get a chance to visualize the things you really like, and they bring positive emotions to your mind.

It is a very easy practice, and there are several tools that can help you. You can listen to guided visualizations whenever you feel anxious, and that would help you in taking your mind off the negative triggers.

When you visualize pleasant scenarios, you are actually able to see them from the eyes of your mind. Seeing is believing, and your mind is able to switch tracks easily. Always remember that positivity is the only thing that can help you in the hopeless darkness of negativity.

Simple emotions of love, beauty, nature, and compassion can help your mind in thinking positively.

The scope of visualization is very wide, and it can become a powerful tool in fending off stress and anxiety.

Emotional Freedom Technique

Most people don't realize, but the cause of most of their physical and mental lies in the imbalance of energy inside them. We are more than just the body. Our emotions, life energy, and physicality work in unique sync. Whenever any part of this system goes out of balance, we suffer as a whole. This is the reason most eastern medicine practices also heavily rely on energy healing. Healing practices like acupuncture and reiki can have a profound impact on correcting such imbalances.

Emotional Freedom Technique (ETF) Tapping also works on similar principles. It is a technique that has been used to treat soldiers suffering from post-traumatic stress disorders, and it has proven to be very effective.

While for acupuncture and reiki, you'll need to go to an expert, you can do ETF tapping yourself anywhere and bring down your levels of anxiety. Even in case a person is going to have a full-blown panic attack. This tapping can help in lowering the level of stress and anxiety and prevent the panic attack.

ETF is very effective, and it is very easy to perform. You can customize the whole process as per your need and feel your level of anxiety going down as you practice it in times of need.

ETF is performed in cycles. With every cycle, you'll have to assess the level of anxiety you are feeling, and you can continue repeating the cycles until you start feeling comfortable.

Through this process, you address the negative emotions that may be contributing to stress and anxiety. By tapping on various meridian points in the body, you allow the energy in your body to flow more freely. This helps in restoring the smooth flow of emotions, and your mood also starts improving.

Studies have proven that restoration of the smooth flow of energy in the body has a very positive impact on the moods and emotions. People who undertake acupuncture treatment experience improvement in their mood after their sessions. When the energy in the body is flowing smoothly, it helps in dispelling negative emotions that get stronger due to blockage in the path of energy flow. The meridian points that you tap help in opening up the neural pathways that can help in the process.

There are 5 major steps to ETF tapping. It is important that you pay attention to each step as every step is important and helps in bringing down anxiety.

1st Step

Single Out the Issue Causing Anxiety

There can be several things that may be driving you towards anxiety. However, if you'll try to address all the things that are making you anxious at the same time, it wouldn't be that effective.

It is important that you identify the strongest emotion that is making you feel anxious at the moment. If there are other stronger issues, too, you can address them separately.

You can enhance the outcome of the process if you address each issue in its own time.

2nd Step

Identify the Intensity of Anxiety

Before you begin ETF tapping, it is important that you close your eyes briefly and try to assess the level of anxiety you are feeling at that moment. Rate your level of anxiety on a scale of 0-10. It is important that you know the level of anxiety before you begin so that you can see the calming effect you are having and know the number of cycles you'll have to perform tapping. If you begin without scaling the level of anxiety you are feeling, you will face difficulty in assessing your progress.

3rd Step

The Setup

ETF tapping follows a two-pronged approach. While the tapping helps in unblocking the neural pathways, the positive and reassuring statements help in making you emotionally balanced.

In the third step, you will have to establish a setup phrase that will help you in addressing the problem, causing stress and anxiety.

This setup phrase should simply have two main portions:

1. It must directly acknowledge the issue you are facing
2. In this statement, you must accept and encourage yourself despite all the problems

For instance, if you are feeling really frightened due to anything, acknowledge your fear in the first part of the statement. In the second part, accept yourself despite your fears and flaws and reassure your mind that you'll come out of it.

Your setup statement can be something like this:

Even though I am feeling scared and anxious, I completely accept myself, and I will come out of it.

I want to run away from all this, I understand I am scared, but I will come out of it, I accept myself.

I am feeling lost at the moment, but I will find my way. I love myself and accept the feelings I am having at the moment.

As an individual, you can have your own setup statement that addresses the most important issue you are facing at the moment. Try to keep the statement simple and more focused. Also, remember that your setup statement should only have your problem as the center argument. Including the problems faced by others doesn't work here. It is not a prayer; it is a way to heal your mind.

4th Step

The ETF Tapping Sequence

In this part, you'll have to tap the meridian point explained below. You can tap the points from your index fingers or your middle finger or both if you like. Even if you want to use more fingers, feel free to do that. The tapping doesn't need to be very hard; remember some parts are sensitive, and it can hurt if you tap too hard. You simply need to stimulate those parts through the tapping so that the neural pathways open up.

There are 9 meridian points that you'll be tapping in this step are:

Hand (Karate Chop): This is the side of your palm below your pinky finger. The part of the hand used for giving karate chops. This is the reason it is called karate chop. Using the fingers of the opposite hand, tap on this surface.

The inner edge of the eyebrows: You'll need to tap at the center of your eyebrows just above the bridge of the nose.

Side of the eyes: This is the outer edge of the eyes where the eyebrows end. This will be the part between your eyebrows and the temple.

Under the eyes: This is the area under the eyes where the hard part of the cheekbone is.

Under the nose: This is the area just below the nose and center of your upper lip.

Chin: This is the area at the center just below your lower lip and above your chin

Beginning of the collarbone: This is the area where the collarbones begin

Underarms: This area is approximately 4 inches below the armpits.

Top of the head: This is the crown of your head. The topmost part.

These are the 9 points that you'll be tapping. You simply need to tap at each point 7 times while you focus on your setup phrase.

In the first cycle, you should try to acknowledge the problem fully. Don't run away from it. If you are feeling fearful, acknowledge that fact. Don't just stop at saying that you are feeling frightened. Bring up all the things that are making you feel fearful and anxious. This acknowledgment helps in changing the perspective about the problem. Once you have acknowledged the problem in its entirety, it loses its punch. When you are acknowledging the problem with its vivid details, the energy system in the body is also gearing up. This acknowledgment also helps in gathering the right amount of energy to dispel fears and anxieties.

In the second cycle of tapping, you can start expressing your intent. Tell your energy system the things you want regarding this problem. Tell the things you want to feel at that moment. Express desires to have the feelings or traits that can help in solving the problems you are facing.

In the third cycle of tapping, simply express your acceptance of the state you are presently in. Good or bad, this is your body. Everything that happens inside you is a part of you. You will have to accept all the things. It is important that you accept yourself as you are.

In the fourth cycle, express some love and compassion for yourself. You surely deserve it. Think of all the positive traits you possess that can help you with this problem. Express the love for the feelings you want to have. Your deep longing to have those feelings. This will help your energies to drive you closer to these feelings.

In the fifth cycle, just be thankful. Gratitude is a very powerful emotion. If expressed with deep emotion is can be overwhelming and has healing powers. Express your gratitude to the cosmos for providing you the power to get through the problems. Be thankful. Think of everything that has helped you in the process.

You should do the tapping sequence as follows:

You should begin by tapping a few times on the karate chop of your hand. You don't need to tap on the karate chop in every cycle. Just begin with it and then follow the tapping sequence in the same order as given below:

1. The inside of the eyebrows
2. Side of the eyes
3. Under the eyes
4. Under the nose
5. Chin
6. Collarbone
7. Underarm
8. Top of the head

You need to complete 5 cycles of tapping in this sequence.

5th Step

Reassess the Intensity of the Emotions You are Feeling

The ETF is a very powerful way to bring down stress and anxiety. However, the impact can be at a different pace for every individual. Therefore, once you have completed the 5 cycles of tapping, relax. Now focus inwards and reassess your feelings once again. On a scale of 0-10, try to judge the level of anxiety you are feeling. The scaling of 0 is great, but anything below 5 is good. If you were feeling really anxious, it might require a few more rounds of tapping to calm you down. But, you should assess your progress after completing the 5 cycles every time.

The ETF tapping has proven its worth in bringing the anxiety down even in people suffering from posttraumatic stress disorders, and hence its effectiveness in lowering anxiety is unquestionable. The best thing about this technique is that you don't need any kind of help, setup, or preparation for doing it. You can even do it while commuting or even in your office.

Neuro-linguistic Programming

Our subconscious mind is very powerful, and it is active more than we can imagine. We don't realize its powers as most of our jobs are done by the conscious mind like learning things, reacting, and things like that.

The conscious mind performs the function of setting the targets. It is the part of the brain which you can influence. The motivational speeches, pep-talks, and morale-boosting stories knock at the doors of the conscious mind. However, this is not the mind that actually does most of the jobs.

It is the job of the subconscious mind to place things deep down in your memory and make them your nature. You don't pick habits consciously; your subconscious mind picks them up for you.

When your intent is set on something, it is your subconscious mind that enables you to become effective in that field.

It is such a powerful portion of the brain that it can take out anything from your brain or put anything in place. The fears, phobias, anxieties, and doubts become a core part of this mind. It doesn't happen overnight. When your mind is constantly training on these things, it is thinking obsessively about these things, or it is forced to experience these emotions, they get embedded in the subconscious mind. As this part of the mind is more powerful and has a greater say, these feelings can start overpowering your functional brain. The best way to get rid of such negative emotions is to train this part of the brain to not think about those things. The problem is that it is not that easy.

While you can influence your conscious brain easily, the subconscious brain doesn't understand the same language. It works on internal maps that are affected by your repetitive behavior in a certain manner and other stimuli like preferred representational system (PRS).

Influencing the subconscious brain is difficult as that would require triggering of the right events repeatedly. This is where Neuro-linguistic Programming can help. Practitioners can help in training the subconscious brain to become biased towards some specific triggers.

Anchoring, rapport building, swish patterns, and visual/kinaesthetic dissociation are some of the techniques through which this task can be accomplished.

Although studies are still going on in this field, it has been found that this therapy can be very helpful in dealing with fears, anxieties, and phobias. It can help people dealing with posttraumatic stress disorders greatly.

Discover the Importance of Deep Breathing

Breathing is an integral part of living. Without breathing, we will not survive even for minutes. The air that you breathe in is responsible for providing life energy.

We all know that, don't we?

Yet, rarely any of us ever takes breathing that seriously. It is something that is happening on its own all the time. It is a task that no one needs to teach us.

However, the air we breathe can do much more than keeping us alive. The way we breathe can have a deep impact on our physical, mental, as well as spiritual well being.

If you start practicing deep and controlled breathing daily, you'll find that your mind has started working better. It would invite fewer negative thoughts and would remain more calm and composed.

Deep and focused breathing requires intense focus. All your attention gets centered on the rhythm of the breathing, and the negative thoughts hovering over your mind lose their effect. Holding the breath for a little longer than usual can have a very calming effect on the mind. If your mind always keeps roaming around and never sticks to a particular thing, you must try it.

You can practice deep, controlled breathing whenever you feel anxiety building up inside you. You don't need any setup or arrangement. You can do it in any position you want. Even sitting or standing in any specific position is not required.

Deep breathing is a very important part of the whole yoga regimen as it believes that for calming the mind and the body, there is no better cleaner than a long and deep breath.

If you ever feel that negative thoughts are overshadowing your mind or anxiety is going to overpower you, please follow the deep breathing routine given below.

You can record it in your own voice and then simply listen to it and follow the instructions whenever you feel anxiety taking over you.

Deep Breathing Routine

Please get yourself in a comfortable position

You can practice deep breathing meditation in any position you like

Whatever is causing stress at the moment is temporary

It will go away

You just need to breathe

If you are sitting at some, let your body relax

If you are in a standing position, ensure that you have ample support

Dep breathing is the most natural thing to do

It is an act that leads to self-realization

You can close your eyes for deep focus

If you don't feel comfortable, keep them open

Fix your awareness at any point in front of you

Now, bring your awareness to your breathing

You don't need to alter or control your rate of breathing

You just need to observe

Breathing is such an easy and simple act

Yet, it is so important

Watch the air fill your nostrils

Observe it getting out

Simply watch the breath coming in and going out

Breathe in

Breathe out

Breathe in

Breathe out

Breathe in

Breathe out

Don't try to change anything at the moment

Keep your awareness focused on the process of breathing

Simply observe the way you are breathing

Let the rate of your breathing stabilize

Breathe in

Breathe out

Breathe in

Breathe out

Breathe in

Breathe out

Now, we will try deep breathing

It is a very simple process

You just need to inhale slowly and deeply

No part of the process needs to be rushed

Just let the breath come in slowly

Try to observe and feel every part of it

You will inhale through the nose to the count of 7

Remain aware of the breath

Hold that breath for the count of 7

Then you'll release it even slowly release the air through the mouth to the count of 10

The process is slow

But there is no rush

You deserve this time

Just focus on your breathing

Start inhaling through the nose

Slowly and deeply

1....2......3......4.......5.......6.......7.....

Keep the awareness focused on the breathing

Now hold this breath to the count of 7

1....2......3......4.......5.......6.......7.....

You may feel the pressure

There might be some stress building up inside you

There is no need to worry

This stress is positive

It is good for you

Now, exhale through your mouth to the count of 10

1....2......3......4.......5.......6.......7........8........9..........10

Very slowly and deeply

You need to really slow in this part

You have to push out as much air as you can

All the air you exhale will take away the stress and anxiety present inside you

It will make you feel relaxed

It will make you feel euphoric

Take a deep breath again

Feel the sensation this air creates at your nostrils

Pay attention to the fragrance it carries

Feel the thoughts that are entering your system with this air

Be conscious of the energy it brings with itself

Follow the path it takes inside you

Now, hold this air for a few moments

Be steady

This is the moment of control

This is the moment of truth

This is the moment of awareness

The pressure building inside you

Tells you that you can surpass anything

You have got that inside you

Now allow this air to pass out slowly through the mouth

There is no need to rush

Let it exit slowly

Let all the used up air go out

Feel the pressure inside you recede

Feel yourself getting engulfed by extreme relaxation

It feels as if a big load has been taken off the chest

Enjoy this feeling for a few moments

Relax!

Again take a deep breath

Start inhaling through the nose

Slowly and deeply

1....2......3......4.......5.......6.......7.....

Keep the awareness focused on the breathing

Now hold this breath to the count of 7

1....2......3......4.......5.......6.......7.....

Now, exhale through your mouth to the count of 10

1....2......3......4.......5.......6.......7.......8........9..........10

Very slowly and deeply

Focus your awareness on your breath

Is it stable now?

Are you breathing at a slower pace now?

Are you still feeling anxious in the same way as earlier?

If you are still feeling anxious

Continue deep breathing for a bit longer

If you feel that your anxiety has come down

Stop controlling your breath

Breathe at a natural pace

Simply,

Breathe in

Breathe out

Breathe in

Breathe out

Breathe in

Breathe out

Breathe in

Breathe out

Breathe in

Breathe out

You can open your eyes when you are feeling comfortable

If your eyes are open

Maintain your position for a bit longer

Just try to feel your surrounding for a few moments

Reflect upon the state of your anxiety

Whatever the reason for anxiety be

Breathing deeply always helps in diverting the mind from disturbing thoughts

You can relax now.

Letting the Train of Thoughts Pass-By

Most of the time, we simply take the fast train to the overthinking land. We don't allow the thoughts to pass by and start participating in them.

Our mind is a very complex organ. In a single day, it can have anywhere between 50000-70000 thoughts. That means we have only a few less than 3000 thoughts per hour or almost 50 thoughts per minute. This is a big number. Do you feel all those many thoughts bombarding your mind all the time?

It happens because the mind is very efficient. However, it also has certain biases. It gives preferential treatment to thoughts filled with sorrow, pain, stress, fear, and anxiety. It does that to ensure that you remain cautious. It is a part of the evolutionary learning that the brain has imbibed.

It may be a good trick for longer survival in the wild where you are exposed and defenseless. It is a very poor strategy for living a fulfilling life in the world. However, the period of certainty and security witnessed by the human mind has been very short, and it has started just a few centuries back. It has endured the periods of tough survival for thousands of years and hence those instincts are still dominant.

Therefore, the mind can consciously suppress positive thoughts and only keep the negative thoughts to the surface. The more you feel identified with those thoughts, the more powerful they'll become.

The only way to escape this sad trip is to give this train of thought a miss. Do not participate in negative thoughts.

If you start having negative thoughts that might lead to anxiety, simply create physical diversions for yourself. Engage in an activity that would require your intense physical participation. It can be a game, exercise, running, or anything else that keeps you busy for the moment. Don't try to engage in any kind of leisurely activity like watching a movie. The more you give your mind the leeway of imagination, the harder it will try to take you on board.

If the thoughts of pain, trauma, or failures of the past appear in your mind, and a link appears to any future event, don't try to argue that. Take it a sign that this discussion needs to end. The mind will drag you down to its desired level and then beat you with experience. Creating a diversion is the best way to ditch falling into the trap.

Relabeling of the Thoughts

Anxiety has a knack of attacking from multiple directions or at least creates an aura like that. When you start feeling anxious, it becomes difficult to understand the exact number of things that are bothering you. The problems look intense, and it starts looking like that you wouldn't be able to bear it anymore.

The best way to fight a stronger opponent is to identify its strengths and weaknesses clearly. Posturing and bluffing is a common war strategy, and many wars have been won like that. Your mind does that on a regular basis, and it is a pro in that game.

Whenever you start feeling very anxious and feel that a panic attack might be nearby, start deciphering the cause of the panic. Try to label the things that are making you anxious.

You need to label each emotion that you are feeling.

Are you feeling scared? Try to identify the thoughts that are making you scared.

Are you worried about the results of something? Try to assess the real importance of that result.

If you are facing difficulty in breathing, remind yourself that you have a panic attack, but it would pass. It isn't anything permanent. It is just a phase. You have been through it several times.

If you are having several thoughts in your mind, label them one by one. Assess them, acknowledge them, and allow them to pass. Letting go of stressful thought works best in such situations. The more you'll try to duck these thoughts, the stronger they'll get in your mind.

Put correct labels on the thoughts, causing anxiety and let them go. Neither hide from them nor try to hold on to those thoughts.

Chapter 7: Productive Habits to Help Get Out of the Deadlock

One of the biggest problems with overthinking is that it leads to procrastination. In fact, the whole point of the brain for causing anxiety is to push you into inactivity. It wants you to stick to a corner so that the risk can be minimized. As we have already discussed, this can be a good strategy for survival in the wild. It is no way to live in this world where your contribution matters.

Procrastination is one of the most common side-effects of overthinking. It keeps you in a never-ending loop of thinking that has no scope of action. Your mind can keep forming strategies and then discarding them after a point to form newer and better ones. This process can be continued until the end of time.

What you really need is a plan to break the chain of thoughts and get into action. The longer you keep thinking, the harder it will get to stop overthinking about it. Even the best strategies in the world can get washed down the drain if they are not put into action.

Procrastination can be one of the biggest negative traits of an overthinking person, and it would also support your habit of not taking action on time.

Given below are 5 strategies that can help you in ditching the thinking mode and taking action. You can pick any of these as per the situation and break the deadlock. Remember, the longer you remain in the deadlock, the harder it will become for you to get out of it.

The 5 Second Rule

Fear has a very deep-rooted relationship with postponing things. When you are afraid of doing something, its results, or have a distaste for it, the mind automatically starts overthinking about it. It makes you think about the consequences if things go wrong and would also make you believe that things would go wrong. Many a time, if you don't act on time, the mind will be able to convince you that the time has passed and there is going to be no use of taking the action then.

The mind likes to keep you sitting tied to thoughts. That's the safest playing ground as per the mind.

We only postpone things for the future that we don't like to do. The things for which we don't feel that passionately or the things that have been forced upon us. The things about which we feel passionate, we prepone them.

People don't want to get up in the morning even though the alarm clock rings several times and gets snoozed. The reason is their dispassion for getting up. They don't feel excited about the prospects of the day.

The same people would get up hours early if they have to do something about which they are really passionate.

However, you can't be passionate about everything you need to do. Especially not about the things you fear or loath. Yet, inaction will only push you into overthinking.

Make it a rule to get into action within 5 seconds of having the thought. It is a very short window. But, you don't need to finish the job in 5 seconds. You simply need to initiate.

For instance, if you need to go to the office, within 5 minutes of the rining of the alarm clock, you must be off the bed. Any longer you stay there, and your first preference would be to snooze it one last time.

Once you cross the 5 seconds window, your mind would start overthinking the whole process and would surely find things to prove the futility of the whole process.

Get into action before it is too late. This is a great way to break the shackles of procrastination.

Ditching the Autopilot

Most of the decisions taken by us are not conscious decisions. They are the decisions taken on instinct. We really don't put much thought into them. This happens because our mind remains on an autopilot mode most of the time.

If you have not been taxing it much about making real decisions, it likes to make decisions based on references. The things you did in similar situations earlier. Did they lead to any negative outcome? What probability of success does it see of for the actions in this attempt?

Your actions are guided by the autopilot in your mind on the basis of such questions. The situations are never judged on their merit. The mind doesn't like to see the probability of the success this time and the conditions that might lead it to the result. It wants to maintain inertia. This is the reason most people procrastinate and never take action. Their mind easily disqualifies most of the possibilities without even considering them a little. The remaining time you'll have at hand now will get utilized for overthinking.

If you want to ditch this trap of overthinking, you must ditch the autopilot. Look at the things mindfully. Take all the decisions consciously. Look at the merit of every situation, and don't try to assume things a lot. This will prepare a better ground for action, and it will also spare you from overthinking when you stop assuming a lot.

Starting Positively

One of the biggest reasons for our backing down from taking any kind of action is our tendency to look at things pessimistically. We begin on a negative note and then expect things to end positively. This almost never works.

The negative thought process is disheartening, and it is bad for the initiative. Chiding your own mind will not pump you up; it will push you into inaction.

Try to start anything new, even a day with positive intent. Don't weigh it down with expectations as that may also fill you with worries. Simply set out with a positive note that things would get better from where you start.

If you feel that looking at things in a positive manner from your perspective is not possible due to your limited view, try changing your perspective. Put yourself into the shoes of someone else you could imagine doing a better job at it. Think it through with a different perspective. Sometimes, changing the perspective can bring all the change in the work. The same things that may look very challenging from your angel maybe a piece of cake for others.

Once a man was looking for a famous church in a village. He had come walking from far and was getting grumpy. He saw a boy paying in the way and asked him the distance of the church. The boy thought for a few seconds and said 24,858 miles. The man was awestruck in disbelief. He said that the church couldn't be that far. I have come looking for it from so far.

The boy said that it was 24,858 miles as per the path he had taken; however, it was only 2 miles if he walked in the opposite direction.

Sometimes we simply look at things from a very difficult angle. Looking at it through someone else's perspective can change the whole story.

It can make the work easy and interesting. If you feel stuck at some work and feel that you don't have a going there, try thinking differently from the angle of someone else.

Acknowledging the Fears

Fears can push us into inaction. It has a very strong impact on our decision-making skills. If we don't address our fears, it will keep cornering us. Even if we keep avoiding the fears, our mind doesn't sit silently; it makes you think all the time only about those fears and consequences of the actions.

There is no escape from this cycle. If you want to avoid it, the only effective way is to acknowledge your fears.

The moment you acknowledge the fears, they lose the deadly impact they have. You are able to clearly understand the kind of impact they'll have. You also get a chance to look beyond the fears and assess the chances of success clearly.

This is a good way to break the deadlock and come out of the habit of procrastination led by fear.

Learning the Art of Setting Milestones

Our mind is constantly looking for the avenues to push us into inactivity. It seeks ways to push you into inaction, as that is the safest approach.

Many people who began working ambitiously at one point end up in failures not because they had put in the poor effort but because their mind was able to convince them of the futility of their actions.

For instance, you aim to lose 30 pounds and get slim. Your aspirations, external motivations, and inspirations can energize you to begin work in that direction. But, it is a task that requires constant motivation as you will be working against your own body. The body would make your work difficult. The mind would assist the body in it.

This means that after a few days, maintaining that motivation can get very difficult. The task of 30 pounds is not something that you are going to get within a few days or weeks, and hence there is a high probability that you'll surrender.

Many people surrender even before they have begun as their mind starts overthinking about the probabilities of success and find none.

Now, think if you had defined your goal in a more accurate way and broken it down into smaller milestones.

You'll lose 30 pounds in 6 months looks like a much well-defined goal. There is a target timeline so that you can't keep postponing it further. This is your first challenge to procrastination.

However, 6 months is a very long period, and maintaining motivation, even with a defined goal, can be difficult.

You also need milestones to help you in your pursuit.

Milestones help you in staging the results in smaller compartments so that you can track your progress.

You need to lose 30 pounds in 6 months means that you have 24 weeks to lose 30 pounds. It brings us to 1.25 pounds per week.

You will have a weekly target, and that can act as your constant motivator. You will have some weeks in which the weight loss would be slower. The milestones would push you to work harder the following week for making up for the deficit.

There will be weeks when your achievements will be higher, and the milestones will pump up to work harder for achieving the final goal faster.

Setting clear goals, dividing them into smaller milestones, and getting into action immediately can help you in breaking the chains of procrastination and inactivity.

Chapter 8: The Wonderful Art of Meditation

Meditation is an amazing way of calming the mind and building the focus in the right direction. Meditation can help in calming even the most agitated minds. It brings clarity of thoughts and helps you look at things from a broader perspective.

Meditation is thousands of years old practice and has been followed religiously in eastern cultures. It is very useful for relaxing the mind, sharpening focus, and increasing awareness. All these three things ultimately help you in lowering anxiety and putting a stop to overthinking things.

Many people think that meditation may increase overthinking as you allow the mind to ponder over things for even longer. However, that's not true as when you meditate, you become more mindful and you are able to look at the problems with considerable detachments.

Detachment makes all the difference in the way we perceive problems. When we feel too identified with the problem, we are not looking deep inside but trying to find an escape root. When you are looking with detachment, you are able to observe the root cause of the problem and that takes you near the solution.

Most of the time, the problems that we feel are very big in our lives have no significance at all. If there was a person who was very cruel or abusive to you in your childhood, there is a great likelihood that he would invoke the same feelings even when you grow up. This can happen despite the fact that you may have grown bigger, more powerful, and wield more authority now.

Do you know how they tie elephants in India?

They dig a small peg in the ground and tie the elephant to it with a thin rope. That role can't keep the elephant tied. Yet, the elephants never try to break that rope. Do you know the reason why?

When the elephants are very young, they are tied with similar ropes. At that time, the ropes are powerful enough to hold them. However, despite the fact that the elephants grow at a phenomenal rate, their mind is never able to grow out of the power of that rope. This is how fears generally work.

Meditation can help you in analyzing the mind and finding irrational fears that might be causing stress and anxiety.

How Can Meditation Help?

Meditation can give you the right process to look at the problems. It will provide you the firm rooting where you won't feel scared of the issues causing anxiety.

It also helps you in addressing the events in the past that trigger anxiety and fear. You are able to unload the baggage of the past and understand the ways in which your thought process works.

It is a very simple practice that doesn't require rigorous training or outside help. You only need to be in constant touch of your own self. The technique is important, but that is only a smaller part of meditation, the bigger part of meditation is your ability to get in touch with your own self. Once you are able to establish a strong connection, the things that cause anxiety don't remain significant.

Meditation is an excellent practice for people who are suffering from stress, anxiety, depression, internal chaos, and fears.

What Kinds of Meditations can Help?

There are dozens of types of meditation techniques that are focused on various goals. Some help you in becoming more mindful while others help you in relaxing the mind completely. There are meditations for making you feel more grateful towards the world, while others can help you in creating resting awareness where your mind can truly rest.

Some important meditation techniques that can help in easing stress and anxiety are:

Body Scan Meditation

This meditation technique is also called a progressive relaxation technique. It helps you in addressing the problems in your body. Stress and anxiety can lead to stiffness and pain in the body. You might find it difficult to complete the usual tasks in the day without feeling the pain. This stress can make you ache for relief. Body scan meditation is a very soothing practice in which you address the areas of pain in your body through your awareness. You acknowledge and accept whatever is causing the pain, and your awareness helps in easing the pain. This meditation technique is very helpful in relieving pain. It also helps in calming the mind and you are able to get a better understanding of your fears.

Focused Attention

This meditation technique uses the breath as the anchor to bring your awareness to a single point. You are able to anchor your mind better, and getting hold of your racing thoughts becomes easy. You can do this meditation anywhere and it is very helpful in case you are feeling frightened or anxious.

You are able to become consciously aware of your thoughts and stop your mind from wandering here and there.

Acknowledgment

This meditation technique is especially very helpful if you are trying to run away from your fears, and they are getting stronger by the day. It gives you an opportunity to acknowledge all the feelings in your mind and accept them. You are able to register everything that's going on inside you and hence the darkness of ignorance fades away.

It is very helpful in clearing the mishmash of emotions, and you are able to note the things that are disturbing you in reality. You must remember that acknowledgment of the problem is the first step towards solving it effectively.

Acknowledgment of the thought also helps you in clearing the clutter in the mind and makes it possible for you to let go of the things that are solving no purpose in your memory.

Visualization

We have already discussed the contribution of the visualization technique in relaxing the mind and bringing the calming effect. With the help of certain imageries, you can distract your mind from the existing negative chain of thoughts and plant a positive message in your mind. Our mind works very efficiently on subtle hints, and hence whatever you feel is easily incorporated in the mind.

Loving-Kindness Meditation

This meditation technique is very helpful in case you are stressed and anxious about certain people. People from our past and present have a deep impact on our life. Some people can have a very deep and disturbing impact on our life. Their actions can leave very deep wounds that may not heal even after years. We form grudges against such people and then get stuck in the cycle of carrying that grudge forever. Simply the burden of the memories keeps the wounds alive forever. We also find it really difficult to trust others or lead a normal life.

This meditation technique can help in getting over such trauma. It gives us a chance to move on in life and make new and better memories. This is one of the best meditation techniques to bring peace in life and heal the wounds.

Reflection

This meditation technique helps in finding answers hidden deep inside our minds. There are several things that we simply assume without applying any logic to them. There are certain fears that have no place to be, but they thrive in our minds as we seldom pay attention to them.

This technique helps you in reflecting on the problems and addressing them in a logical way. You get a chance to reflect upon the perceived problems and lower the burden of stress and anxiety on your mind.

Resting Awareness

In this meditation technique, you don't fight your thoughts, you allow the thoughts to enter but don't get affected by them. You maintain a resting awareness of the thoughts and observe their genesis and end. This can help you in getting out of the clutches of your disturbing thoughts that overpower you anytime.

How to Practice Meditation?

People have strange notions about meditation. They feel that to
mediate; you need to sit in specific contorted postures for hours
and chant mantras that you don't understand. Meditation is a
way of life. It can be practiced in any form and posture you like.
There are some simple rules that you must follow as they help
you in building focus and prevent you from falling in the trap of
negative emotions.

When and Where to Practice

There are certain meditation practices that help in lowering
stress, and they can be practiced anytime you feel stress and
anxiety taking over your mind.

Certain meditation practices like the body scan meditation work
best when you can get in specific positions. Like the body scan
meditation should be carried out at the end of the day lying flat
on your bed or a mat. Loving-kindness meditation should be
practiced early in the morning for making you feel better
throughout the day. Keeping such things in mind can help you in
getting the most out of your meditation practice. This doesn't
mean that these meditation techniques can't be practiced at

other times of the day. It only means that during these times, they are more effective.

Duration

There can be no diktat about the duration of meditation practice. In the beginning, you may face problems even in sitting straight for 5-10 minutes in a stretch. The mind would be very volatile, and it would keep tripping you down. However, as you practice, you get used to the routine, and you are able to meditate for much longer without losing your focus.

The duration should be as per your convenience. However, in the initial days, you should try to progressively increase the duration of your meditation sessions. It is said that if you practice meditation continuously for 48 hours around the same time, your body gets used to the routine, and you would face no difficulty in making it a part of your life.

Posture

Some people have great apprehensions about the sitting posture. They feel that they can't sit in cross-legged postures for too long. Some people that they can't sit in cross-legged posture at all due to health issues or their weight.

You can practice meditation sitting in a cross-legged posture, sitting on a chair, lying down, standing, walking, and running. It is your focus of the mind that matters the most and not the way you fold your legs.

Sitting in a specific posture like the cross-legged posture definitely has a positive effect. There are certain pressure points that get pressed, and they help in maintaining greater focus and awareness. However, your inability to sit in those postures should prevent you from getting benefits of meditation at all.

Pro-Tips

Always Keep Your Spine Straight

This is one of the most important rules that you must follow while meditating. Either you are practicing meditation in sitting, standing, or lying position, your spine should always be straight. You shouldn't be bending sideways or slouching to your back or leaning forward. Not keeping the spine straight will affect your focus and may make you feel distracted, sleepy, or even fearful.

For instance, leaning forward while meditating can lead to the formation of depressing thoughts. Your anxiety levels would shoot up, and you'd find it very hard to remain focused on any particular thing.

Bending backward will make you feel restless.

If you tilt to your right, you might start feeling sleepy. Tilting to your left may lead to an increase in your sexual desires, and hence focus on the mind would get difficult.

You Can Use a Backrest

If you are practicing meditation in a seated position, you can use backrest to keep your spine straight. Supporting your spine is not a problem in meditation. You only need to ensure that your spine remains upright, and you don't bed your back.

Don't Use a Neckrest

Using a neck rest is very bad in meditation, as in that case, you will lose control of your thoughts. You have to keep your neck straight and you can't use a pillow. Your neck needs to remain unsupported if you want to have active control of your thoughts. Using neck rest also creates the danger of drifting into sleep.

Rest Your Hands Comfortably

You can rest your hands in a comfortable position. There is no need to keep them on your knees or in any other specific position.

Don't Overstress Your Body and the Mind

Meditation is a relaxing activity, and it shouldn't become a punishment for the body or the mind. You must practice meditation only for as long as you feel comfortable. Practicing 5 minutes more than you usually practice is not a problem but forcing yourself to practice for hours can prove to be counterproductive.

Even if you want to increase your meditation time, break it into smaller parts if your body or the mind is not feeling comfortable. In place of having an hour-long session, you can have two sessions of half-an-hour each. Your aim should be to achieve greater balance, focus, and awareness.

Meditation is an age-old, time-tested way to bring clarity in mind and increase awareness. It can help in lowering anxiety and stress levels. If you feel troubled by your thoughts and your mind has fears that come to haunt you anytime, meditation can provide you the answers to most of your problems and you must definitely give it a try.

Chapter 9: Negative Thoughts- They Aren't Invincible

There is no way we can eliminate negative thoughts from our minds. They are a part of the defense mechanism of the mind, and they are important. However, the problem begins when they become so important that everything else starts losing its significance. The negative thoughts can start overpowering you and push you in the swamp of self-pity and regret.

These thoughts are destructive and very damaging. They begin with positive intent but cause a lot of damage. They can shatter the victim's self-confidence and make recovery very difficult.

People with negative thoughts find it very difficult to summon the courage to get out of the trap. It may be difficult, but it is definitely doable. It is very much possible for everyone to get out of the trap of negative thinking.

The common problem with negative thinking is that people have the wrong approach. They are unable to identify the negativity in their thinking. You can't fight an enemy you can't see. This chapter will help you in identifying negative thoughts and give you ways to get out of their trap.

Recognizing Negative Thinking

Negative thoughts mostly begin as good intentions. Like, 'I should eat healthily.' There is no problem with this statement. But this statement has most likely come from regret. One makes such a statement when there is a realization that there are problems in the lifestyle that need to be changed. These statements stem from the compulsion one feels. However, making such statements can have a negative impact on your psyche. When you say that you should eat in a healthy manner, you are indicating that there is a problem that needs to be corrected. Such problems are never easy to deal with as they have a long past and mostly take a lot of time. In the meantime, your brain would keep getting guilt signals every time you fail to keep up to your pledge.

There would be times when you wouldn't be able to keep up to your resolve at all, and that would have negative consequences. The negative thought process would get stronger and it would keep pressing you down at the back while you don't even recognize it.

This is just one statement. You can put pledges regarding your relationships, habits, thought patterns, fears, phobias, or anything else, and the result would be the same. Whenever you won't live up to the demands, there will be negative thoughts of self-pity, regret, and resentment.

It soon gets converted into patterns of automatic negative thinking. The mind learns and starts reacting to things in negative ways even before an action has taken place. It means you start losing wars even before you have declared them and even keep getting ridiculed for losing a war you didn't even fight.

Negative thinking doesn't have a grand beginning.

It begins with smaller failures and keeps building up inside your mind. It is important that you change the way you look at things. The way you make commitments to yourself has a very deep impact on your mind. When you say that you should do something, it implies that there is a need to do something, and you must get on to it. It becomes a compulsion to follow that up. Now, most such things are important and they must be done but it is always not possible to do them. In that case, you will be carrying an unnecessary debt on your mind.

You must make such statements carefully. In place of saying that you should eat healthily, you should say I will try to eat as much healthily as possible from now.

The same should also go for your fears. If you are fearful of public speaking, but your work forces you to do that, there is no use saying I should be able to speak in public without fear. This statement will fill you with self-pity as you'll fail yourself every time you speak in public. You must start with something like I know I am not able to speak in public with confidence but I am working on it. I will try to find ways to get over this problem.

Negative thinking can have a detrimental impact on your confidence and self-respect. It can make you feel bad all the time, and most of your efforts may go in vain as you would keep feeling defeated from within.

However, if you are already suffering from negative thinking, there are several coping strategies that can help you.

Coping Strategies

Mindfulness

Mindfulness is a great way to get out of the vicious cycle of negative thinking. Mindfulness helps you in remaining grounded in reality. You are able to understand your limitations clearly and get a chance to work slowly toward improving them. Mindfulness is a process of continuous improvement. It also helps you in getting free from the baggage of past experiences, and hence you are able to try fresh every time.

You can try mindfulness meditation to prevent the formation of negative thoughts in your mind.

Thought-Modification through Cognitive Behavioral Therapy

Cognitive Behavioral Therapy is based on the concept that our feelings, actions, thoughts, and physical sensations are interconnected and changing one can help in changing others.

It can help you in reducing stress and coping with complicated relationships. You may find it easier to deal with grief in life or face other tough challenges in life.

This is a way to modify the way our conscious mind work. This therapy doesn't have any effect on the subconscious mind, but it is able to affect the way our conscious mind thinks and perceives things.

Chapter 10: Developing a Winning Mentality

A winning attitude is something that we develop. It is a result of the right conditioning. The same people who look so uber-confident and enthusiastic can become just the opposite of they develop a negative mentality, and the same is true vice-versa.

If you want to get out of the trap of negative thought processes and develop a winning mentality, you will have to bring some positive changes in your personality.

Given below are some small yet important changes that you must make in your day to day personal life and personality to develop a winning mentality. These changes are not very significant, yet they can leave a very deep impact on your conscious brain and the way it perceives problems. This is a thing which will matter a lot when it comes to having a winning mentality.

Start the Day with Positivity

This is a point we have already discussed in earlier chapters, but it can't be stressed enough. The way we start the day has a very deep impact on the way it will end or at least go for the most part.

If you woke up late and from the very beginning, you are worried that the day is going to be bad, you can be sure that you are correct because you have set the tone for the day. On the other hand, if you wake up smiling and leave your home expecting good things to happen, you will have many pleasant surprises in the day.

This is not some magic. When you are in a pleasant mood, even simple things look good. Have you ever felt the way day feels when you have received some very good news? On the day you are in a bad mood, even the best of the weather would mean nothing to you.

This doesn't end here. Your mood is constantly affecting your psyche. It is shouting loud and high that everything is going wrong. It has already accepted that the day has gone wrong, and it is going to end on a worse note. It would take a miracle to lift up such a mood.

Start your day on a positive note, and try to maintain it as far as possible. It would have a positive impact on your mentality.

Focus on Positivity Daily- Find at Least 4 Positive Things of the Day

At the end of the day, daily try to find at least 4 positive things about the day that has just come to its conclusion. This should be done without exception.

It can be anything that you liked on the whole day. You saw a flower, and it looked beautiful enough to lift your mood, mention it. You met a stranger who smiled at you genuinely, that can be a thing to mention. You helped someone in any way that made you feel food; this can be a thing to mention. It can be anything you liked but there should be at least 4 things that you liked about the day.

If you like, you can even journal then in a dairy or just say them out loud. This simple act can help in changing your perspective about the world. You start looking for positivity around you.

Do Something Positive for Others Daily

This is a simple act of kindness that you may do. It can be a minor act. It doesn't have to be anything major every day. But, you must do one thing at least every day that made any difference to the life of one person. When we do some act of kindness, we not only touch the lives of others, but the selfless act also touches a corner of our self too and lifts our spirit and mood.

It fills you with a sense of happiness and you feel proud of yourself either other people acknowledge it or not. It is a change that can help in infusing positivity in your mind.

Live in the Moment

You must learn to live in the present. You must stop reflecting too much on the past. Live every experience as it comes, and please stop judging things on the basis of your past experiences. This will give you a fresh perspective. Change is a reality and constant truth. The only thing that is constant is change. When we judge things on past experiences, we are coming in the way of this change.

Appreciate Yourself

This is important. You must learn to appreciate the genuine qualities in yourself. You must try to look for strong points in your personality and work on developing them. The more you appreciate yourself for your qualities, the easier it would get to break the negative thinking process.

Appreciating yourself is important if you really want to be successful in your relationships, job, and life in general. The people who are not even good enough in their own eyes can never expect to be good enough for others. If you don't appreciate yourself, you'll keep feeling stressed and insufficient. There will always be a problem with your overall satiety levels.

Find Avenues to Remain Motivated

Remaining motivated is important. You must find all the ways that are there to remain inspired and motivated. From movies to ted-talks, whatever works for you should be used to get the required push. Motivation keeps giving you the boost to continue working with the same force.

Work on Your Body Language

It is important that you work on your body language. From your clothing to the way you conduct yourself, everything in your personality should speak of your confidence and positivity. You must remember that positivity and negativity both are contagious. A positive person can light up the whole room while a negative person can make the people around gloomy. You should pick the type of person you want to be.

Remember that it is more important for you than it is important for others. Your attire, appearance, and conduct all have a deep impact on the way your mind functions.

Appreciate and Be Grateful More Often

Make it a general rule to appreciate others even for minor things that help you or make your life easy. It is another positive change that can help your mentality a lot. When you are saying positive things about others, you are reminding your mind to think in the same way. When you are expressing your gratitude for others, you are being more open, accepting, and acknowledging. This has a very deep impact on your conscious mind.

Look for Positivity Even in Grim Situations

This is a no brainer. You can't lose all hope when things start to go south. A big part of winning mentality is to maintain composure even in grim situations when others are losing hope. It is an art that needs to be developed.

Look for Solutions and Not the Problems

You must look for the problems and not the solutions. This is a statement we often hear. However, as soon as things get out of control, our mind starts looking for escape routes or even better starts exaggerating the problems. We don't contribute anything; on the contrary, we end up making things worse.

All this happens because our mind remains focused on the intensity of the problem and not on the solution. You must remember that thinking about the problem and the amount of damage it can cause can never solve it. You will have to start thinking about the way to resolve it. It is a talent that will need to be cultivated.

Conclusion

Thank you for making it through to the end of this book, let's hope it was informative and able to provide you with all of the tools you need to achieve your goals whatever they may be.

Overthinking is a problem that largely remains ignored. There was a time only a few people were affected by this problem, and its extent was not very high as people generally remained busy with other tasks at their hands. However, thanks to modernization people now have more time and fewer things to do. A big chunk of the time now gets utilized in overthinking. The high rate of anxiety disorder in society is a solid testimony of the fact.

The intent of this book has been to put all the facts related to overthinking in front of you and explain their causes.

I have tried my level best to make this book as comprehensive as possible in giving the details of the ways in which you can stop overthinking and by bass the effects of stress and anxiety.

This book has also tried to explain solutions like deep breathing, EFT tapping, mindfulness, and meditation so that you can make use of them in your personal life.

You can also get all the benefits of the process by following the simple steps given in the book.I hope that this book is really able to help you in achieving your goals.

Finally, if you found this book useful in any way, a review on Amazon is always appreciated!